# R.G. Smith

12
NH
3037
VF 114
NAVY

# The Man and His Art

# R. G. Smith

## AN AUTOBIOGRAPHY

with Rosario "Zip" Rausa

**Schiffer Military History**
Atglen, PA

Book Design by Robert Biondi.


Library of Congress Catalog Number: 98-88370.



Printed in China.
ISBN: 0-7643-0755-X

We are interested in hearing from authors with book ideas on military topics.

Published by Schiffer Publishing Ltd.
4880 Lower Valley Road
Atglen, PA 19310
Phone: (610) 593-1777
FAX: (610) 593-2002
E-mail: Schifferbk@aol.com.
Visit our web site at: www.schifferbooks.com
Please write for a free catalog.
This book may be purchased from the publisher.
Please include $3.95 postage.
Try your bookstore first.

# Foreword

Many are considered, but few achieve the designation of "Living Legend." One such genuine, widely acclaimed and self-effacing person is the foremost artist of military scenes in the world: Robert Grant Smith, known affectionately as "R.G." His paintings and drawings grace the walls of the Pentagon, the National Air and Space Museum, and the National Museum of Naval Aviation, among others. They also adorn the offices of high government officials, military officers, and those who just appreciate fine artistry. Wardrooms at sea, headquarters ashore, and military bases around the world enjoy and take great pride in their "R.G. Smiths" on display.

The wonderful works of art presented in this book did not result from R.G.'s formal art education. Rather, they were created by an aeronautical engineer who became a self-taught artist. As a configuration engineer in the days before and after World War II, R.G. was called upon to design and illustrate aircraft then being conceived. The results of his design efforts are incorporated in such remarkable airplanes as the SBD Dauntless, A20 Havoc, AD Skyraider, A3D Skywarrior, A4D Skyhawk, and F4D Skyray. Even with all the praise he has received for his artistic achievements, R.G. still considers himself foremost an engineer. This stems from his long association with the Douglas Aircraft Company (later McDonnell Douglas). This organization has produced many outstanding aircraft for the armed services, but principally for U.S. Naval Aviation. The SBD, AD, A3D, and A4D were clearly "best in class" worldwide, and made their mark as such in the crucibles of World War II, Korea, and Vietnam, as any Naval Aviator of the times will attest.

Although his major contributions to aeronautical engineering are remarkable, it is his consummate skill as an artist which propelled him to the pinnacle of respect and admiration he now enjoys. His trained eye for aeronautics and his abiding respect for those who fly, especially in combat, enabled him to portray the spirit as well as the image of aircraft. His dramatic, realistic, and often soaring backgrounds of sky and clouds attract any aviator's eye, and make that flyer feel at home when viewing his paintings. Clearly, R.G.'s creations have been instrumental in the preservation of the proud heritage and rich history of Naval Aviation.

R.G. was not solely an engineer and an aviation artist. He served two tours as a combat artist for the Navy during the Vietnam War. He captured the essence of warfare in Swift boats engaged in firefights in the Mekong Delta; the tedious but absolutely essential handling of huge volumes of ordnance and supplies; and the hazardous flying of close air support for the ground troops. As to carrier operations on Yankee Station during the war, no one depicted them with such compelling force as R.G. Smith. He considers his works of the Vietnam period one of his greatest contributions. The Navy and personnel who served in the combat zone agree with him. More than once he took weapons in hand and participated as a combat sailor, as well as an artist. R.G. described his Vietnam combat experiences as one of the highlights of his life.

The superlative quality and immense quantity of R.G. Smith's works are notewor thy. For example, more than a million of his lithographs of commercial and military aircraft have been printed. The Navy recruiters once published 150,000 copies of a R.G. Smith "litho" to assist in recruiting.

Testimony to his distinguished achievements are the many honors he has received. In 1972 he received the Salmagundi Club's Louis E. Seley Award for "outstanding achievement in the field of oil painting." In 1979 the Navy's Flight Demonstration Squadron named him an Honorary Blue Angel. In 1987 he was given the Fighter Hawk Award for "Countless, Enduring Contributions to the Art, Science and Safety of U.S. Marine Corps Aviation." He received the American Society of Aviation Artists Franklin Mint awards twice, once in 1989 at the U.S. Air Force Museum in Dayton, Ohio, and in 1991 at the Royal Air Force Museum in Hendon, England. In 1987 the U.S. Naval Institute presented him its Award of Merit. In 1994, he became the first recipient of the R.G. Smith Award, named in his honor, by the National Museum of Naval Aviation in Pensacola, Florida. The Boeing Company (formerly McDonnell Douglas) sponsors the $500 annual award for excellence in Naval Aviation art. The Naval Aviation Museum Foundation had a bronze bust created of R.G., and it is a featured attraction at the Museum.

R.G.'s most treasured award, however, was his designation as Honorary Naval Aviator No. 10 in 1973, an extraordinary accolade considering only nine other individuals had received this prestigious honor since the first was awarded in 1949. As the Deputy Chief of Naval Operations for Air Warfare, I had the privilege and honor to make this designation at a ceremony in Long Beach, California.

As R.G. enters his golden years, we will miss the remarkable and stirring paintings we have come to expect from his pallete. It so happens his grandson, Steve Tack, inherited R.G.'s artistic talent, and has produced some exceptionally fine aviation art on his own. Steve also aspires to become a combat artist for the Navy. His mother, R.G.'s daughter, Sharlyn Marsh, claims the artistic talent skipped a generation and descended on her son, Steve Tack. However, she has undertaken the herculean task of locating, cataloging, and photographing as many of the 1,500 to 2,000 R.G. Smith paintings and drawings as can be found. The imprecision of the number is evidence of R.G.'s generosity and positive attitude toward public service. He has many times produced spectacular paintings only to give them to admirers, with no accountability. Mrs. Marsh has been complimented and encouraged for her work by Dr. William Dudley, Director of the Naval Historical Center and VAdm. Don Engen, USN (Ret.) Director of the National Air and Space Museum. They note that Sharlyn's effort is a most valuable contribution to aviation art history.

To paraphrase James Michener's famous phrase from his Korean War novel, The Bridges of Toko Ri, "Where do we get such men?", we might ask ourselves, "Where do we get such families?" The answer is, at the R.G. Smith's homestead.

Vice Admiral William D. Houser, USN (Ret.)
Arlington, Virginia 1998

# Contents

# Acknowledgments

The chief engineer of this autobiography has been our daughter, Sharlyn Marsh. Her inspirational support, drive, organizational ability, and devotion to the task have been remarkable and are deeply appreciated. Shar's son, Steve Tack, an artist in his own right, provided dialogue of an invaluable transcript of his lengthy interviews with me. My old friend, Vice Admiral Bill Houser, USN (Ret.), was instrumental throughout the production of this book. His historical knowledge, personal efforts at locating my paintings at various museums, arranging photography of them, and providing dynamic support all along the way, have been great beyond measure.

I am especially indebted to the following three men: Hal Andrews, Harry Gann, and Peter Mersky. Author, historian, and aeronautical engineer, Hal Andrews, a contributing editor of several aviation publications and one of the comparatively few individuals designated an Honorary Naval Aviator, applied his profound skills in reviewing the narrative, ensuring accuracy. Harry Gann, another in the prestigious list of Honorary Naval Aviators (there have been only 24 people so designated since the designation began in 1949), a long-time personal associate at the Douglas Company, engineer, aviation historian, and writer, and for my money, the best aerial photographer in the business, lent his most helpful expertise to the manuscript. Peter Mersky, editor of Approach magazine and a highly regarded aviation historian/author with numerous well-received books to his credit, also lent his expert eye to the narrative.

Many others helped make this book a reality. They include: Gail Munro and Lynn Turner of the Navy Combat Art Center; Harvey Krasner, Charles Cooney, Captain Richard Knott, USN (Ret.), Captain Ted Wilbur, USNR (Ret.), Morgan Wilbur, Sandy Russell, Ken Smith, my son Rick Smith, Dee Unruh, Sue Henderson, Captain Don Florko, USN (Ret.), Carol Mason, Fred Rainbow, Editor of U.S. Naval Institute Proceedings; Mike Machat and Bill Westerman of the Boeing (formerly McDonnell Douglas) company, who assisted in obtaining key slides of some of my paintings. Captain Steve Millikan, USN (Ret.), editor of Hook magazine, provided his support. Captain Bob Rasmussen, USN (Ret.), Curator of the National Museum of Naval Aviation, Jean Tarnok, and Captain Earle Rogers, USN (Ret.), Vice President for Education and Editor of Foundation, the voice of the Naval Aviation Museum Foundation, were instrumental in gaining photos of my paintings on display at the museum.

Special thanks go to Vice Admiral Don Engen, Director of the Smithsonian's National Air and Space Museum, who, with the assistance of Dominic Pisano and Captain Tim Woolridge, provided photography of my paintings displayed at the museum, and to Kathy Glockney and the staff of NAS Patuxent River, MD.

I must add it was Shar who convinced me that retiring doesn't mean quitting. Her encouragement breathed life into a career the chapters of which I was ready to close. Hidden in the attic, garage, closets, and under beds were countless numbers of my paintings and drawings, long since forgotten. Shar matted and framed over 350. Helped by Sue and Jim Willoughby and Bob Hallenbeck, her efforts led to an exhibit of a retrospective of my works at the Phippen Museum in Prescott, Arizona, in 1996. I also want to thank John and Vicky Kloes, who traveled the eastern seaboard from New York to Pensacola, Florida, helping to locate, photograph, and document my works which were on display in various collections at museums and other facilities.

R.G. Smith
Rancho Mirage, California,
1998

Dedication

To my loving wife Betty and to the military heroes who wore their uniforms with pride and went into battle on foreign soil in defense of our country so that we might enjoy the freedom and the fruits of this great land.

Betty and I in our Rancho Mirage, California home. We have had a wonderful life together.

# Introduction

The Association of Naval Aviation is honored and proud to have provided administrative support during the production of this autobiography of Robert Grant Smith. Better known as "R.G." Smith, he is a Naval Aviation legend, a superior patriot, and a distinguished artist of the highest order.

R.G. considers himself a configuration engineer first and an artist second. He has excelled at both vocations. Even though he participated in the design of some of the Navy's most well-known and highly regarded airplanes, it is his compelling depictions of them through art which has captured our attention for nearly six decades.

His masterful works, which include commercial aviation and aviation subjects of the other military services – not to mention a magnificent collection of non-military art – will endure. These paintings, drawings, and sketches will most certainly continue to excite and enlighten the generations which follow.

ANA salutes R.G. Smith!

Richard C. Allen, Vice Admiral, USN (Ret.)
President

# THE MAN

After scrutinizing a number of my paintings, which featured skyscapes and a variety of cloud formations, an art critic seemed to have me all figured out. My motivation for such dramatic renditions, he noted, emanated from an inner soul which harbored angst and tension. According to Webster's, "angst" means "a gloomy, often neurotic feeling of generalized anxiety and depression." I hated to disappoint the critic, but the simple truth was, I liked to paint clouds. That's all there was to it.

I'm a stranger to angst, and while I have encountered a fair measure of life's tensions just like most folks, true tension to me is what you feel riding a Navy patrol boat at night along a jungle river during a fire fight in South Vietnam. I experienced this, and it remains one of the genuine highlights of my life. Yet it had nothing to do with my inclination to portray a gathering of thunderclouds on canvas. I just like to paint clouds. And airplanes, of course, not to mention landscapes of the far West, native Indians, and nudes, among a few other subjects.

• • •

I was born on May 7th, 1914, at our home on North Boylston Street in the Boyle Heights area of Los Angeles. When I was a year-and-a-half old we moved to Oakland. My uncle Will had built a small house on Damuth Street in Oakland for himself and his wife, Maude, and then helped build one for us a short distance up the hilly street. For a time we stayed with my aunt and uncle. We had a creek in the back, and although we had running cold water in the house, we supplemented this with forays to the creek where we collected water in buckets and hauled them to the house. We had to heat hot water on the stove. Very simple living.

After leaving my aunt's and uncle's, we rented a place on Randolph Avenue. I attended McChesney Grammar School until 1920 when we made the move into our newly completed home on Haddon Road. There I attended Cleveland Grammar School, where I skipped a semester in both the second and third grades. McChesney was considered a bit more advanced than Cleveland, and I had already learned much of the subject matter.

I had two sisters, Grace, five years older, and Jane, who came after yours truly. Jane and I were very close, and shared a sort of wry and sardonic sense of humor throughout our lives. Jane passed away last year, and I still miss the correspondence and phone calls we exchanged on a regular basis.

My dad, who was in the insurance business, was a great fisherman and outdoorsman. We spent a lot of time together fishing and camping, most often in the San Joaquin Valley. We had no sleeping bags or tents, just blankets and branches, which we broke from the trees for bedding. If it rained we slept in the car. My love of the outdoors, I suppose, comes from this early exposure to nature in the raw. Because of that love as a youngster, I initially wanted to become a forest ranger, but that dream was to be short-lived.

During the early years in our new home finances were tough, and we went without a lot of things that kids take for granted. I remember asking my parents for a bicycle for my tenth birthday, a request they could not afford. They did, however, manage to fund a new scooter, the type you propel yourself with one leg while the other rests on the base of the scooter. Once you got going you could put both feet on the scooter. One day, I came barreling down the hill to our house and tried to execute a turn into our driveway. I didn't quite make the turn, and crashed into a retaining wall that paralleled the driveway. This mishap resulted in a two and a half inch lesion on my forehead. As soon as my mother saw me, she was horrified and rushed me to the doctor's office for stitches. Before starting his procedure, the doctor handed me a mirror and said, "It's not very often that a ten year old gets a glimpse at his own skull." Later, my mother marched me down to Capwell's, where she exchanged my prized scooter for a new book, The Outline of History, by H.G. Wells. I began reading it, and was captivated by its contents. Almost instantly I became a devotee of history. I was especially fascinated by the Civil War, and have been a buff of the conflict between North and South ever since.

A second major milestone in my life occurred on May 21st, 1927, when Charles Lindbergh flew solo across the Atlantic in the "Spirit of St. Louis." I was only 13, but Lindbergh's achievement ignited in me an immediate and, as it turns out, unending interest in aviation. I just had to get into this world of flying. Ironically, I did not want to become a pilot. Rather, I wanted to design and build aircraft.

In those days, my youthful companions and I didn't have modeling kits, but we could buy chunks of balsa wood, ambroid (quick-drying glue), and certain model aircraft sections, such as plastic wheels. From these rudiments we created our own designs and model airplanes.

Someone discovered that balsa was used as a kind of shock absorber for lumber carried on some of the ships that came into the harbor on the east side of San Francisco Bay. We hustled down there one day, scrounged around, and found a block of balsa covered with tar. In exchange for half of the block, a friend with a band saw cut away the tarred sections and sliced up the remainder for us. We had a great time creating airplanes from that section of balsa. We were especially adept at making gliders.

On occasion, to my parents' chagrin, we used to empty the powder from firecrackers and insert it into the bottom or along the fuselage of the models as a propellant. Sometimes we arranged a firecracker with a fuse on the model and squeezed out most of the powder so it would burn slowly. We flung the aircraft skyward and watched it fly until it exploded in the air with a sharp and noisy bang. The fragments of balsa and wire fluttered to the ground. My mom and dad would have a fit, because we had spent days making a model only to blow it up with the firecracker. I suppose there's a streak of violence in most of us.

One day, an Eaglerock biplane crashed at the local airport, killing the two pilots. The wreckage was stowed behind the hangar. I asked the airport manager if we could have some of the wreckage. He gave his permission, so we foraged through the debris and came up with a set of rudder pedals and a control stick. We gathered up other items and constructed a wheeled vehicle with airplane-type controls, mainly using the rudder pedals for steering.

We moved our creation to the top of a hill on Haddon Road. Our coaster-wagon was positioned for launch with me at the controls. In our ignorance, we believed the rudders would control direction on the ground as they did in the air. Not true, as I learned moments later. I started down the hill, and after a short distance of travel the wagon began to veer off the straight-away, despite my persistent application of rudder opposite to the veer. I never did get back to the middle of the street, but instead continued to roll toward the bottom of the hill, where I smashed into a cast-iron hitching post for horses, complete with an iron replica of a horse's head mounted on top. The post was stronger than the wagon, which was damaged beyond repair and struck from the inventory. Fortunately, I was not hurt. Clearly, my knowledge of aerodynamics in those days was lacking, but we sure liked those flying machines.

As kids we also played "street football" on the same hilly incline. As soon as one team made a touchdown we switched directions. If you scored going uphill, you played defense on the downward slope.

I spent my days outdoors involved in one activity or another, but at night I liked to draw. We had no television in those days, so my evenings were spent either reading history or drawing, mostly airplanes.

When I was 13, the local newspaper published one of my drawings. It depicted an Indian on a horse. I never dreamed that this was the first of a lifetime of drawings and paintings that would be published or reproduced.

In high school I was active in sports. At 145 pounds, I was considered too small to play football, which was my favorite sport, but I did letter in basketball, soccer, and track. I also wrote a sports column for our school newspaper, The Aegis.

After graduating from high school I made a little money painting signs for grocery stores and other businesses. I had a knack for it. Recognizing this, my folks asked if I would prefer art school, or engineering training.

We examined the possibilities and settled on engineering, specifically mechanical engineering. Aeronautical engineering courses were in their infancy and not available at many schools. The Polytechnic College of Engineering was only three miles away. It was especially appealing because, if I signed on as a janitor, I could attend tuition-free. It was a three-year school for a bachelor's degree (with a two-year program for an associate degree). I didn't care much for rising early and hustling down to the school to clean the rest rooms, blackboards, and erasers, along with other mundane but necessary chores, before reporting to class. Interestingly, my high school friends who opted to study engineering at the University of California in Berkeley used to borrow my books and engineering notes. They felt that the courses of instruction at Poly were a bit more advanced than their curriculum at Cal.

So, I studied mechanical engineering and took some aeronautical engineering courses. Since the field of aviation was relatively new then, California didn't offer a degree in aeronautical engineering.

I was also active in sports during my college years. By then, I weighed 165 pounds and was big enough to play halfback on a semi-pro football team sponsored by the local Piedmont Merchants. We were actually good enough to play against the team that scrimmaged against the East team, as a preliminary to the famed East-West game. This annual contest was played at Kezar Stadium in San Francisco. We lost to this team by a single touchdown. I also lettered in basketball and crew (as a coxswain) while in college.

As to romance, I dated very little in high school. It certainly wasn't lack of interest in girls, but more a shortage of funds, and the fact that I was basically shy. My best friend in high school was Kenny Jones. I dated his sister Madeline a few times mainly because they lived close by and we were all good friends. During our senior year, Kenny introduced me to the pretty freshman he had been courting. Her name was Betty Coler. My first impression was that, even though she was good looking, her long blonde hair was messy and disheveled. I didn't really pay much attention to her until she and Kenny broke up and I found myself looking for excuses to stop by her house to pay her a visit. Even though she only lived about three blocks away, our backgrounds were worlds apart.

I came from a family of very modest means. We were a close-knit family, and we all pitched in when something needed to be done. My mother ran a "tight ship," and also saw to it that we were all present at family meal time. Her maiden name was Stella English. She was raised in Pennsylvania, where there still remains a town called English Center named after her family, which settled there sometime in the mid 1800s. Her father, Orange English, fought at the Battle of Gettysburg during the Civil War and returned home minus the use of his legs.

My father, who sold insurance most of his life, was quite politically motivated. He ran a successful campaign for the infamous John Davies, who won by a landslide and became mayor of Oakland. Subsequently, dad was appointed Chief Food and Market Inspector for the city of Oakland. During that tenure, we always had an abundance of food in the house. My dad's lineage, incidentally, has been traced all the way back to George Washington's army.

Betty, however, grew up under much different circumstances. Her mother, Doris, daughter of Julia and John Parker Palmer, was educated in both England and the United States. During her youth, she made 13 trips to Europe, often sailing with Captain Smith, with whom her parents had become close friends and who subsequently went down with his ship, the Titanic. The Palmers owned newspapers in England and the U.S. Doris, their only child, was indulged by her father, nurtured by her mother, and raised by a governess. She was very bright, strong-willed, and spoiled.

Against her parents' wishes, Doris ran away and married her lover, Charles Joseph Coler, a man her parents considered far beneath her.

Little is known about Betty's father. He died in 1918 at the age of 32, during the great flu epidemic, and just prior to the birth of his third child, a son. Like me, Betty was the middle child in a family of three. Within three months of the death of her husband, Doris lost her father to diabetes. Both widowed, she and her mother were now left to fend for themselves and raise three young babies. Doris, who had had lifelong exposure to the newspaper business, soon landed a job writing fashion columns for the Hearst newspapers: "To The Queen's Taste," by Doris, and "Just Between Ourselves," by Dore'. In the meantime, Betty's grandmother was managing the household and raising the children.

While writing for the Hearst newspapers, Doris met and married James A. Murray, a cousin of Millicent Hearst's and the head of classified ads for The San Francisco Examiner and The Post Enquirer, two of William Randolph (W.R.) Hearst's newspapers. They bought a beautiful home on Radnor Road in a posh neighborhood overlooking Lake Merritt. They often traveled to San Simeon as guests of W.R. and Marion Davies to attend W.R.'s famous costume parties. They hob-nobbed with the stars: Jean Harlow, William Powell, Charlie Chaplin, and others. On rare occasions they would sojourn to Southern California with W.R. and Marion for a weekend at Marion's home in Beverly Hills or her beach house in Santa Monica.

By the time Betty was a teenager, her mother was not only writing her syndicated fashion columns, but she also published two magazines, The Oakland City Women's Club Magazine and The Men's Athens Athletic Club Magazine. Consequently, Betty saw very little of her mother and stepfather, except when they entertained at home.

As they were growing up, the children were usually fed in the breakfast room, supervised by the cook or the Filipino house boy, both of whom assisted their grandmother with many of the parental duties. Betty was a very serious student, maintaining straight A's in her academic courses throughout high school. She loved her grandmother very much, and always felt that she, rather than her parents, was the backbone and mainstay of her family life.

We went on our first official date on April 16, 1933. I took her skating around Lake Merritt, and then to see the new blockbuster movie, King Kong. From then on, it became a fairly routine date on weekends for us to take in an afternoon movie, a 65-cent dinner at the Robinhood Tea Room, then another movie at night. Although Betty never shared my enthusiasm for sports, she did attend some of my football and basketball games, and got quite a thrill seeing my crew throw me into the water after a victory in a rowing competition.

One of the things I liked most about Betty was that she seemed unaware of the differences in our backgrounds and life styles. She didn't seem to care that I couldn't afford to take her on expensive dates or that I didn't have the funds for the material things she was used to. On the contrary, she seemed to enjoy the simple things, like coming to dinner at our home on Friday nights where our family always dined together.

In the meantime, completion of a thesis was required in order to get my degree. In a joint effort with another student, we designed an airplane and an engine for it. The aircraft resembled a World War I type biplane powered by a Liberty engine.

I graduated from college at 20 with a B.S. in mechanical engineering. The stage was set, and I was anxious and determined to start designing airplanes, and not at all worried about finding a job in aviation. I should have worried.

It was the tail end of the depression, and although I had written every known aircraft company in the region offering my services, I got zero responses. Aeronautical engineering opportunities in the San Francisco area were almost non-existent.

Consequently, I signed on with the Work Progress (later, "Projects") Administration, the W.P.A., a program established by President Franklin D. Roosevelt. The program was designed to provide useful work for the otherwise unemployed, building roads and bridges and promoting creative arts.

At the initial interview the man in charge said, "You're just out of college, is that correct?"

"Yes," I said.

"OK, then," he said, "we'll give you that desk over there. We'll bring some stuff for you to do."

I went over and sat down. For three days straight I sat there, but no one brought me work to do. I was not comfortable getting paid for doing nothing, feeding from the government trough, so to speak. I gave up and went home. It was while doing electrical wiring on a temporary basis that I heard people were needed to work a gold mine up north, so I signed on immediately.

Some friends of my folks owned the mining rights to a small area on a fork of the Feather River north of Sacramento. A dam, built 40 miles up river from the site, slowed the water flow to ten percent of normal capacity, which exposed a number of river bars. As the river turns, the velocity of the water flow changes, and deposits of sand and gravel, like a sand bar, piled up along the edges of the turning water. The gold was in the river bars.

We worked several of the bars, shoveling dirt and gravel onto a platform where others heaved the material into sluice boxes. Every Friday we cleaned out the sluice boxes, separating gold from the useless debris. The yield would usually fill a small Mason jar, which was taken to San Francisco, where it was sold for cash. I earned a dollar a day for my labors, which wasn't bad considering I was provided a sort of poor man's room and board: three squares and a cot to sleep on. During the warm summer nights, we slept under the stars.

One of my jobs was to kill rattlesnakes. The country was alive with them. Some curled up at night to sleep on the warm, dusty trail which extended from the camp to the river bars. In the morning, I went ahead of the others to clear the way. I averaged killing one each day. I once sent a box full of rattles to Betty, who was not at all pleased. She promptly gave them away to a friend, who made a hat band out of them.

After a time, the state authorities announced they were going to open up the dam and let the water through. Subsequently, I moved on to a mine near Quincy, California. The mining engineer on this job reasoned that the old mother lode, the main channel that distributed gold along the Sierras, had broken in several places in the last 100,000 years, and that a mammoth channel, or at least part of it, might still be accessible. He wanted to carve a tunnel into one area, figuring he would run into the promising main channel, which would then be easy to work. In the designated area, we began digging a tunnel six feet high and six feet wide. After probing inward 200 feet we encountered volcanic clay. This was a promising sign, but, unfortunately, the clay was saturated with water, and chunks of wet ceiling began falling down on us, obviously a hazardous condition. This brought the project to an abrupt end.

Speaking of ends, I almost came to an end myself one day in the tunnel. We had stuffed dynamite into five holes, each three feet deep, to blast out some of the earth in the tunnel. We lit the five separate fuses so that they would all reach the dynamite at approximately the same time. We had slow-burning fuses which, once lit, burned about two feet per minute, giving us ample time to get out of there. All of a sudden, one of the fuses took off – whoosh! It was fast-burning! We dropped everything and ran as fast as we could. We reached the mouth of the tunnel and had just turned away from it when the explosions rocked the area. A close call!

After a year, my gold-mining venture came to an end. I returned to Oakland, where I worked odd jobs once again, mainly painting "specials" for a meat market and a couple of grocery stores along Athol Avenue.

Sometimes, I painted the price of pork chops on the window front, other times I inscribed a special price for ham on butcher paper. There were 15 or 20 specials a week, so I made some walk-around money doing that. Not exactly art, but in those days every dime counted.

Although I had seen very little of Betty during my employment in the mines, we wrote to each other regularly and resumed dating as soon as I returned to Oakland.

Betty had graduated from Oakland High and entered nurses training, while I continued my efforts to hire on with an aircraft company.

In any case, I got my break for entry into the world of aviation through a most unlikely event: a traffic ticket in the southern part of the state.

• • •

It was 1936, and I was still doing odd jobs in Oakland after my gold-mining adventure. "Doc" Thomas was my dad's good friend and fishing companion. The good doctor's brother, Lloyd, was a police officer in Los Angeles. Doc Thomas told his brother about the son of a friend who aspired to get into the aviation industry. Officer Thomas, the brother, was a huge, imposing man, all of six feet, six inches tall, but he had a soft heart.

While on traffic patrol one day he stopped a driver for speeding. The driver turned out to be the chief draftsman at the Northrop Aircraft plant, a man named Roy Brown. At the time, Northrop was a subsidiary of the Douglas Aircraft Company, and eventually became the El Segundo Division of Douglas.

Officer Thomas told Mr. Brown about me and my desire to get into aeronautics. Under the circumstances, Mr. Brown was predisposed to listen to anything Officer Thomas had to say.

"Send him out and I'll talk to him," said Mr. Brown. Officer Thomas, with silent approval, tore up the ticket.

That led to my visiting Los Angeles, meeting Mr. Brown, and getting signed on with the Northrop company as a blueprint trimmer for $18 a week. Without my degree the pay would have been $16 weekly. Even though it meant leaving Betty behind to finish her nurse's training, my foot had edged open the door, and I was pleased as punch.

I found accommodations for $35 a month (room with a small bunk bed, plus board) with the Lloyd Thomas family. I also threw in a couple of drawings I had done of early California missions. For transportation to and from the plant, I rented my mother's car for a modest sum. Lloyd, Jr., who later became a policeman like his father, was my roommate.

In those days, every part of every military aircraft was drawn separately. Northrop was developing the BT-1, a small dive bomber for the Navy, which was a predecessor to the venerable SBD Dauntless. There were about 50 people working in engineering. At the time, I was low man on the totem pole, which was no surprise.

A multitude of detailed blueprint drawings of the various components of the aircraft were needed. Three copies of each blueprint were required, one for the shop that designed it, one for the files, and one for the customer, in this case the Navy.

Blueprints came off a printing press in big rolls that had to be trimmed and folded in a certain way. I used shears for cutting, and manually folded the sheets to a 9-by-12 inch size so they would fit into the Navy's filing cabinets.

I also performed what was called "detailing." For example, the pilot's seat consisted of numerous component parts. Each one of those parts had to be drawn separately on paper. Then, an "assembly drawing" was created, which portrayed all the parts of the seat on a single sheet. As a detailer, I didn't create any designs. Rather, I copied what the original designers produced. My routine was such that one day I might be detailing the pilot's seat and the next I was trimming blueprints.

I became very familiar with the pilot seat in the BT-1 (I had also done drawings relative to the experimental version of the plane, the XBT-1). My first detail drawing at Northrop depicted a small bushing. It was part of the apparatus that allowed the pilot to adjust the seat up and down using a bungee system, pretty much like the pilot seats in many aircraft today.

Northrop couldn't afford to construct a full-size mock-up of the BT-1, so I was assigned to make drawings which were one-quarter actual size. Consequently, we did much of the mock-up on paper, with dimensions 25 percent of the actual aircraft's size.

We spread the paper out flat on a table. I was more or less in charge, because all drawings had to go through me before they became part of the mock-up. If I discovered an error, for instance, where a drawing didn't match up properly with the part it was to depict, I alerted the head draftsman, who would resolve the matter.

I didn't do mock-up work exclusively of course. Rather, I continued with my other chores, trimming blueprints and executing detail drawings as necessary. Ours was a rather loosely run operation in the sense that we went where we were needed, when we were needed.

One day, I was making a layout of the windshield for the BT-1. I had "cut" a hole in the windshield drawing in order to accommodate the bomb sight. I "phantomed" in an outline of the sight. A phantom line is a long line with two dashes followed by a long line, two more dashes, and so on. This distinguished it from the other lines. A phantom line indicated where an item went through a bulkhead or some other section.

Ed (Edward H.) Heinemann, who was responsible for seeing that the drawings were properly completed, looked at the windshield rendition for a moment, then said to me, "You'd better erase that outline of the bomb sight. If I'm not mistaken, that's a classified item."

That got my attention, and I promptly confessed to drawing a similar picture of the airplane in my leisure time at home. Moreover, I said, "I think I included the bomb sight on it as well."

Ed, who was destined to become a legend in his own time as chief engineer of Douglas Aircraft's El Segundo division, said, "I think you ought to bring it in so we can get a look at it."

It was a simple pencil drawing with a presentation of the bomb sight included. When Ed saw it he decided to confiscate it, "just to play it safe."

I wasn't concerned about the drawing itself, but fooling around with classified material was another matter. The picture disappeared, but a few days later, Jack Northrop showed up in person and handed me a picture of the XA-16 (forerunner to the A-17), an aircraft which never went into production. He gave this to me by way of apology for having to take the BT-1 drawing.

As it turned out, Northrop and Heinemann needed a drawing of the BT-1 to take to Washington with them for discussions with the Navy about the aircraft. I was asked to draw a picture of it. They didn't want a blueprint type presentation, but an actual drawing. Apparently, Northrop and Heinemann liked the art work in the confiscated rendition and wanted me to apply what skills I possessed for this drawing. Therefore, I stopped my blueprint trimming and other tasks and produced a drawing of the BT-1.

It was well received, and led to better things for me. Shortly thereafter, I was assigned to a small room with three other engineers to work on designs.

One of the engineers was a "weight man," that is, his job was to calculate the weight of the various aircraft components. Another was an aerodynamicist named A.M.O. Smith, a Cal Tech graduate. The third, John Wheatly, was also an aerodynamicist. The latter two became long-time and very highly regarded experts with Douglas. My job was to make drawings of an engine, six inches larger than the current one proposed for the BT-1. When questions developed relative to the shape of the cowling for this new power plant, I proposed a fairing which would enhance the appearance as well as the aerodynamic shape of the aircraft. The higher-ups bought the idea. Unbeknownst to me at the time, this modification was to change the scope of my job and shape the future direction of my engineering career.

Not only was my foot in the door of my chosen field of endeavor, the door was opening wider. My new job didn't preclude trimmer/detail duty altogether. I still filled in with detail work and trimming when the occasion dictated.

In the meantime, during my first year at Douglas, I had another close call with death. I received word that my mother was ill and had to be hospitalized. I can't recall the nature of her illness, but it was resolved soon after I arrived in Oakland. After spending a couple of days with the family I scheduled myself on an afternoon flight back to Los Angeles, allowing plenty of time to return to work on Monday morning.

Just prior to departure, an airline customer agent asked if I would be willing to leave a half hour later. A wedding party had requested a last minute booking, and in trying to accommodate them, the airline was asking some passengers if they minded taking the next flight out. "Sure," I said, "it makes no difference to me."

It surely did make a difference to me, for shortly after my return to Los Angeles, I heard on the radio that my original flight had crashed, killing all on board. My heart sank upon hearing the news, it was such a shock and terrible tragedy. I called home immediately to notify Betty and my family in Oakland that I was OK. Thankful to have dodged another close brush with death, I was also very surprised at the hero's welcome I received upon my return to the office the next day.

During that first year I made several weekend sojourns to visit Betty, who was nearing completion of her nurse's training. On one of these trips, during the summer of 1937, we decided we didn't want to spend anymore time apart. Since I was now making enough to support the two of us, $32 per week, we decided to tie the knot. We were married on September 16, 1937, in the Chapel of the Flowers in Berkley. It was a simple but elegant wedding, planned by her parents, and largely attended by their friends and associates. I remember W.R. Hearst giving us a check for $250, which seemed like a fortune to me.

Betty and I settled into a little rented duplex not far from the plant with our new family addition, a German shepherd named King. Our first child, Sharlyn, came along in 1939, and Rick, our son, was born in 1942.

During that summer of 1937, Jack Northrop designated Ed Heinemann as his chief engineer. The clouds of war were brewing in Europe, and in anticipation of the potential market for combat planes, Northrop was developing a multiengine observation and attack plane called the Model 7B. The French government, in particular, was interested in the aircraft. Tragically, on January 23, 1939, during a single-engine fly-past, the 7B crashed at Mines Field (later, Los Angeles International Airport), killing its Douglas pilot, John Cable, and the French representative in the rear. Nevertheless, the French were still interested.

During further evaluation, a French pilot complained he couldn't see the wing tips from the cockpit. Ed Heinemann – we called him "EH" by now – asked me to make an engineering drawing depicting modifications which would resolve this "visibility" problem. The tail and wing didn't change, but we pretty much altered all the other components. I "raised" the cockpit 12 inches, lowered the position of the engines to underneath the wing, and modified the shape of the bomb bay doors so they were parallel to the top portion of the fuselage, among other things.

Heinemann told us, "I'm very concerned about showing these changes to the boss (Donald Douglas). A lot of money has gone into this project, and now we're proposing significant modifications." Despite his concerns, Heinemann still had to respect the pilot's criticisms of the plane, which prompted the changes. After carefully examining the configuration I had drawn, he approved it.

Fortunately, at that time Douglas was having notable success with its DC-2 and DC-3 transports. Perhaps the company's cash flow would be sufficient to cover the modification costs. That weekend, Ed trooped over to the Douglas home and met with the namesake of the company, who was lounging on the deck by his swimming pool. Ed sat down and they talked. Ed explained the problems we had encountered.

"OK," said Donald Douglas, "you've presented the problems, the wing tip and so forth. What's the solution?"

Ed told us later that he was shaking in his boots when he showed Douglas my drawings containing the changes we had proposed. In a way, we had redesigned the entire aircraft. But Douglas liked what he saw, and in the end, told Ed simply, "Go ahead."

I'll always remember the smile Ed wore when he came in that next Monday. He was a very happy man. The airplane became the DB-7, for the French, and later on the British bought it, and the U.S. Army Air Corps, as well. The A-20 attack bomber evolved from this same basic design, and eventually led to development of the well-known, low-level bomber of World War II, the A-26 Invader.

About this time, I was named Proposal Drawings Engineer, and my pay was boosted to a hefty $35 a week. My job was to create a drawing of what an aircraft might look like based on specifications provided by the chief engineer, specifications meaning performance requirements.

These "specs" actually came from the customer, the Navy or Army Air Corps. The services would tell industry what kind of performance it sought from a fighter or bomber, and we in the industry tried to produce the proper design to accommodate them. The specs would go to the aerodynamacists (we used the term 'aero,' referencing them in a collective sense). Aero would produce the basic criteria. Working with the weight engineer, basic figures such as aspect ratio (the ratio of the wing span to its mean chord, chord being the straight line intersecting a wing profile at two points), engine size, landing wheel configuration, etc., would be turned over to the Proposal Drawing Engineer, yours truly. I would then draw the shape of the plane, meaning a configuration that reflected the detailed information provided by Aero, with inputs from the weight people.

There was a lot of give-and-take in these early stages of the design process. We didn't have computers, of course. We made our calculations with slide rules and trial and error: cut and paste. The aspect ratio might have to be modified to reduce weight. The fuselage might have to be more oval-shaped than round to accommodate other components, and so on.

A former associate at Douglas, Ken Smith, reminded me of a strange but unusual event that occurred in 1938 and which amplifies the emphasis on careful handling of classified material in those days. Jack Northrop personally assigned me the task of executing detail drawings of a number of components on an aircraft that was not identified to me. I did the work, turned the drawings in, and despite my curiosity, let it go at that. It wasn't until 42 years later, in 1980, that I finally learned what aircraft the drawings were for. The answer: Project No. 9, a Flying Wing Bomber. Three companies were competing for the contract, including ours. Specifications for the flying wing had apparently been set forth by the government. A .8 scale model of Project No. 9 was built and wind tunnel-tested, but it never went into production. However, the project did reflect some forward thinking in terms of aeronautics, circa 1938.

EH came into our office one day in late 1940. He said, "Ray Raymond, (A.E. Raymond, Douglas Corporation's' Vice President of Engineering – Douglas' senior figure in engineering) is going to be in Wright Field in mid January to talk to the Army about the A-20's successor. He'll need drawings to show them."

Wright Field, in Dayton, Ohio, was a major Army facility. The Air Force was interested in a beefed-up A-20, but Heinemann persuaded officials to look at a new design. EH didn't feel the A-20 could be modified to do the job. So, we designed a bigger, more powerful bomber.

I labored over the drawings Christmas Eve and all Christmas Day to make the deadline. I created what we called three-views – views of the aircraft in profile, from directly overhead, and head-on. Performance data accompanied the drawings. These drawings were the first of the aircraft which became the A-26 Invader. Even though I drew the preliminary design of the airplane, the A-26 was the result of a great team effort by our group.

The A-26 resembled the A-20, but in many ways was far different. It featured side by side seating for the pilot and bombardier (the A-20 had a single-pilot cockpit), and a rear turret station for the third crew member. It also featured the more powerful Pratt and Whitney R-2800 engines, which were longer than the Wright Cyclone R-2600s on the A-20. The R-2800s, consequently, were configured so that the props spun just ahead of the cockpit area, rather than nearly abeam, as in the A-20. The bottom line was the U.S. Army Air Force liked what it saw. The A-26 was soon in production, and eventually became a mainstay among the Air Force's World War II airplanes.

As I said, much of what we did in those early days was trial and error. The vertical stabilizers, for example, were designed as much for appearance as anything else until we learned that by configuring them with a dorsal fin, airflow across the stabilizer was smoother. The DC-2 and DC-3 didn't have dorsal fins at the outset of their life cycle, only later on.

Immediately after the Japanese bombed Pearl Harbor I visited the draft board, fully intending to enlist in the service. To my surprise, I was told I might be exempt because I was married and had a child. I told the board I still wanted to enlist.

"You are doing critical work for our nation's defense," I was told. The decision was made by Douglas' management and the Navy that I was more valuable staying where I was, rather than going into uniform. While I was pleased to be part of the defense industry during the war, I regretted being denied the opportunity to serve my country in uniform.

We were in a constant state of flux in those days. World War II had begun, and aircraft carriers and tactical planes were going through a transitional period. They were becoming more sophisticated in design and functional capabilities.

In the case of the SBD Dauntless scout bomber, I drew eight different tails (during flight tests) before the final one was selected. The test pilot tried each of the versions before we settled on the best one. The changes were hardly more than adding a piece of metal, hammered out on a shaping block, then installing it on the aircraft.

With respect to the Navy aircraft which operated from the rather hazardous seaborne runways known as carrier flight decks, control of a plane on approach was, and still is, especially important. For instance, I drew numerous modifications which entailed adding more size to the stabilizer or rudder to enhance stability under such conditions.

We could overdo it, too. The XSB2D-1 Destroyer was a prime example. Intended as a follow-on to the successful SBD Dauntless, too many "experts" injected their ideas into this aircraft. We went from the SBD's conventional, "tail-sitting" landing gear with two main mounts and a tail wheel, to tricycle gear – two main mounts and a nose wheel – so that the fuselage sat roughly parallel to the ground. Someone else wanted the bombs mounted internally in a bomb bay, instead of externally. As a result of these and other "innovations," the Destroyer got so heavy it couldn't perform, and never went into production. At one point we referred to it as "the lead balloon."

There was a silver lining in this experience, though. What we learned ultimately manifested itself in development of one of the greatest aircraft of all time, the AD Skyraider.

During the golden years at Douglas Aircraft – the late 1940s through the 1950s – the most successful aircraft we turned out were the embodiment of fundamental simplicity. There was nothing fancy about them. They just did the job and did it well. The AD Skyraider was a fine example of this, although it took some doing to achieve its fundamental simplicity.

The AD had many sobriquets, including Able Dog, The Big Machine, Pedigreed Pulverizer, Flying Dump Truck, and Spad. It was a workhorse that could carry immense bomb loads and stay in the sky forever. It remained in the Navy inventory for more than 20 years, and the Air Force flew it extensively in the Vietnam War. However, as with all airplanes, we had some problems with it early on.

One day I was pouring over one of the early concept drawings trying to find places to save weight. I noticed the specs called for a gravity-feed type oil tank, one capable of supplying oil to the engine in a 20 degree climb, which meant it had to be configured above the engine.

A three-inch diameter line would probably be needed to accommodate the necessary oil flow to the big R-3350 power plant.

It would be better, I figured, to have the oil tank installed below the engine, forward of the fire wall. This would allow moving the cockpit 18 inches further forward, save weight, and allow better positioning of the main fuel tank, which was a cell situated directly behind the pilot. In effect, this led to a "step," creating more space ahead of the firewall. These modifications enhanced the overall strength of the aircraft, particularly in the tailhook area, where brutal loads were imposed during "traps" aboard the carrier.

Initially, we had some difficulties with rudder "buzz" in the Skyraider. Airflow around the tail at high speeds created a slightly unstable condition which had to be corrected.

One day, Eugene "Gene" Root, chief aerodynamicist for Douglas El Segundo in 1944, told us, "We just got word that the Focke Wulfe-190 flies beautifully at high speed." American forces had captured one of these German fighters, and the Army was test-flying it at Wright Field in Ohio. The engineers noted that the 190's horizontal stabilizer was situated further forward than the one we designed for the Skyraider. Therefore, Gene Root figured the answer to the XBT2D-1's (the early designation of the aircraft that evolved into the AD) rudder buzz problem was location of the horizontal stabilizer. Although there was considerable disagreement about this, we moved it forward. I managed to position the rear spar of the horizontal stabilizer and the front spar of the vertical stabilizer so that they "tied together," strengthening the structure of the entire tail assembly. (A spar is a structural member running along and "carrying" the ribs of an aircraft wing or tail section.) This cost some extra weight, but paid off by correcting the Skyraider's buzz problem.

Not long after we moved the tail forward, Ed Heinemann, Gene Root, and Leo Devlin (senior engineer at Douglas, and the man I always felt was the (silent) power behind the throne) traveled to Washington to sell the Navy on the AD. Unfortunately, we had designed the XBT2D using the proven R-2800 engine, but the Navy informed Ed and his team that all the remaining R-2800s had been allocated to the Air Force.

Consequently, Ed proposed the Navy allow Douglas to apply funds remaining from another program (the BTD) toward a "new" airplane. The Navy said go ahead, but EH and his team had to have the design ready by nine o'clock next morning. The three men worked through much of the night and produced a design featuring the R-3350 engine. This lengthened the existing aircraft about four inches, but at minimum sacrifice of weight. They met the deadline, and the Navy liked what it saw. This bought Douglas time for further development and design of the plane.

Legend has it that the Skyraider was designed overnight in a hotel room. That's an exaggeration. The basic design was, for the most part, completed before EH and his associates reached Washington. Through the night they primarily made the necessary modifications of the aircraft we had already been working on to accommodate the larger and more powerful R-3350.

The airplane became one of Douglas' most successful, with 3,180 of them built through early 1957. The AD performed heroically in the Korean and Vietnam Wars.

• • •

The D-558-1 Skystreak was hardly more than a jet engine with wings. It wore a distinctive coat of bright, red paint. Some called it "The Crimson Test Tube." It was a simplified research aircraft designed to explore the heretofore unfamiliar regime of high-speed, high-altitude, transonic flight. Its colorful hue made the plane easier to see at the new heights at which it was intended to fly.

Wind tunnels of the day were not very sophisticated. Shock waves generated in wind tunnels tended to "bounce back" and play havoc with the data-gathering process. Actual flight in the unexplored regions near 40,000 feet and at sonic speeds was needed in order to more rapidly develop aircraft, which were now being propelled by jet engines, as well as by reciprocating power plants. It was late 1945, the war was over, and it was easy to sense that jet technology comprised the wave of aviation's future.

Work on the Skystreak began in 1944. Specifications called for it to take off and land on its own power, carry a pilot and 500 pounds of test instrumentation, and achieve the maximum speed possible with an existing power plant, the 5,000-pound thrust G.E.TG-180/J35. The engineers feared the pilot would not survive a conventional bail-out, so we designed a jettisonable nose section which included the cockpit. The pilot took to his chute once the parachute-retarded nose section reached a sufficiently slow speed after its separation from the disabled aircraft.

We reduced risks and uncertainties by keeping the plane as conventional as possible. We configured it as a low-wing/straight-wing monoplane with a cylindrical fuselage designed around a nose air intake and bifurcated air ducts forward of the cockpit. Engine air flowed through the aircraft to the tailpipe or exhaust section.

Initially, we designed a clear, bubble-like canopy, but after low-speed tests, we installed a high-speed canopy with a hooded covering and a flat V-shaped windshield. It was so narrow that pilots had to wear chamois leather covering over their helmets to prevent scratching the canopy.

Playing a part in the design of the Skystreak was a joyful experience. Moreover, it led to a vital milestone in my life. As it turned out, the Skystreak was less important to me for its aeronautical particulars than the fact it inaugurated a relationship with the man who, more than anyone else, influenced my life as an artist. He was Lieutenant Commander Arthur Beaumont, U.S. Naval Reserve, the embodiment of that milestone.

The DD-558-1 was an attention-getter because of its pioneering mission – and its color. The Navy wanted a painting of it, so Lieutenant Commander Beaumont was asked to visit El Segundo for that purpose. I must digress and give some background on this remarkable man and artist.

He was born in England in 1891, but later moved to America. He studied art in Los Angeles, San Francisco, London, and Paris, and ultimately settled in Southern California. He earned a reputation as a superb watercolorist. His maritime scenes were especially popular. He was on active duty for a year or so in the 1930s, having received a reserve officer commission as a lieutenant through the good offices of Admiral William D. Leahy, whose portrait Beaumont had painted, among other flag officers of the time. Off and on through the years that followed, Beaumont did a multitude of paintings for the Navy, many of them of ships of the line. He was energetic, totally professional, and liked to work "on location." He thoroughly researched his subjects. He was innovative, as well. He participated in Operation Deep Freeze in Antarctica. Where others saw only white and blue in this frigid area, Beaumont found wonderful color and conveyed same in his art. He added alcohol to his paints to prevent them from freezing as he worked in sub-zero temperatures for 30-second intervals, retreating to a warmer area before going out again.

He was affiliated with the Navy in some capacity or another for 45 years, and was once described as "Artist Laureate of the Navy."

His forte was painting ships. He demonstrated attention to detail. He figured if a sailor noted a rivet out of place in one of his paintings, he would hear about it. Yet, because of his rather loose style, he had a special ability to convey a warship forging through the rough seas with a feeling of action and dramatic flair.

I first saw him sitting on a bench in the hangar with the Skystreak, painting with his custom-made pallete in hand. His pallete was larger than the normal size and uniquely designed for Beaumont by a destroyer sailor. The recesses for the colors progressed in special sequence from one end of the pallete to the other – "cooler" colors, such as blue, green, and purple – were at one end, with the warmer tones – red, orange, and yellow – at the other.

Beaumont was tall and slim with graying hair. He was dressed casually, but had a kind of flair about him which was manifested in his paintings of ships, for which he had earned an outstanding reputation. His free-wheeling style captured the drama, color, and romance of stately ships forging through the high seas. As I found out later, he was a most affable man, very comfortable in teaching and talking art to others.

I watched him as he worked, mixing paints and executing strokes on canvas as he intermittently studied the sleek research plane. He was facile as he worked with his watercolors, and I thought, "That couldn't be too complicated a task."

"Do you mind if I watch you work?" I asked him.

"Not at all," he said congenially.

I was soon enthralled with Beaumont's techniques. With sure strokes, he applied blue to color the top of the bright red airplane! I didn't say anything at the time, figuring Beaumont was off his feed or something. He then began mixing blue with the red, and other colors as well. I thought, "If it were I, I would use red paint to paint a red airplane." This guy was using blue and other hues, along with the red. I was puzzled.

Yet, the overall effect was as striking as the Skystreak itself. When he was done, the test plane was red, to be sure, but Beaumont saw in its image a variety of other colors to which I had been blind. Somehow, he fused blue and other colors along the edges of the red, which highlighted rather than softened the red. He created a portrait of clarity, beauty, and realism.

"Do you do any teaching?" I asked Beaumont.

He looked up from the easel and said, "As a matter of fact, yes. Every other weekend or so, I meet with a group of doctors who like to paint. We go down to the harbor in the Long Beach-San Pedro Bay area, and I conduct a kind of seminar."

"I would very much like to participate, to join the group, if that's possible," I said.

"Be glad to have you," said Beaumont. I got his phone number, and while I didn't realize it at the time, I had reached a turning point in my life. Those weekend days at the edge of San Pedro Bay were to become my training grounds as an artist. Indeed, I was destined to learn more about painting from Beaumont than I could ever have hoped to learn from a formal course of instruction.

Back to the Skystreak. I should mention that as active as I was in its initial development, once the Skystreak took to the skies in 1947, my cohorts and I were already busy on the next project. While the Skystreak was breaking speed records this side of Mach 1, we were working on its successor, the D-558-2 Skyrocket.

We had entered the fast-moving era of aviation. The Skystreak had reached the threshold of supersonic flight, and the famed Chuck Yeager broke the sound barrier in the Bell X-1 in October 1947. In November 1951, the Skyrocket became the first aircraft to fly at twice the speed of sound, with legendary NASA test pilot Scott Crossfield at the controls.

The Skyrocket had swept wings, one of the most notable differences from its predecessor. Interestingly, the technology that led to this came from the Germans. They had lost the war, but when it came to technological innovation, they were ahead of us in many ways.

Back in May 1945, a Naval Technical Mission had gone to Europe and researched captured German aerodynamic reports. A team of American experts, including Douglas aerodynamacist A.M.O. Smith, went into one plant area where the GIs had pulled out drawers and dumped documents onto the floor and in the passageways. A.M.O. Smith came across data on high-speed wings produced by Dr. Alexander Lippisch, a German scientist. Lippisch had studied delta-shaped wings and related information that Smith determined was valuable. He bundled it up and brought it back to Douglas. EH and others carefully sifted through the newly confiscated data. One of the upshots was the swept-wing design later incorporated in the Skyrocket.

To compensate for the limited thrust then available in turbojet engines, a rocket engine with enough fuel for two minutes of initial flight was installed to complement the 3,000-pound thrust J34 in the Skyrocket. The Reaction Motors four-chamber rocket engine, fueled by alcohol and liquid oxygen, provided 6,000 pounds of thrust for a limited period.

We designed the D-558-2's fuselage with greater diameter and length than the D-558-1 to accommodate the regular and rocket engines. It had the pilot's jettisonable compartment, side-mounted air intakes versus the nose inlet and bifurcated ducts on the Skystreak, and the jet engine exhaust beneath the fuselage rather than at the tail.

The aircraft handled "sluggishly" on the first flights (without the rocket engine) because of a lack of power. Visibility from the clam-shell cockpit, which was flush with the fuselage line, was poor; and directional stability was questionable. We raised the cockpit, designed a flat V-shaped windshield, and increased the height of the vertical tail over a foot. The rocket engine came on a little later with expectations of solving the power problem. However, the decision was finally made to air-launch the D-558-2 from a mother ship, a P2B-1 (B-29), rather than having it take off from the ground under its own power. Progressive flights led, ultimately, to Crossfield's Mach 2 achievement.

Interestingly, one of Ed Heinemann's favorite aircraft, the D-558-3, never got beyond the design study stage. But we thought it would reach Mach 9, the hypersonic speed range. It was as sleek as a bullet. The Navy wanted it, but had no funds for it. The Air Force took the lead in the matter, which led to competition won by North American, which eventually produced the X-15.

At this point in my life, I was thoroughly enjoying my work with Douglas. I derived great satisfaction from transforming specifications into the actual design of an aircraft and giving it form. As the years rolled by, through a kind of osmosis, I was gaining a deep-rooted, from-the-ground-up knowledge of the "anatomical" nature of aircraft. This would manifest itself in my art, but I certainly wasn't aware this was happening at the time. And it didn't matter whether the aircraft was as slender as a dagger, like the Skystreak and Skyrocket, or one with a stocky physique like the F3D Skyknight, a comparatively slow but functionally sound fighter that took to the skies in March 1948.

Late in 1945 the Navy was pursuing a jet-powered, two-seat (side by side), carrier-based night fighter. It had to be able to detect an enemy aircraft traveling at 500 miles per hour as high as 40,000 feet from a distance of 125 miles. The man in the right seat handled the radar, navigation, weapons switches, and other chores.

If the Skyrocket was a speedster, like a nifty running back in football, the Skyknight was a sturdy lineman, laboring in the trenches. It became the first carrier-capable jet night fighter. On a November night in 1952, a Marine flight crew bagged a North Korean Yak-15, marking the first kill in a jet-versus-jet night aerial combat. It had longevity, and was flown on missions in the early years of the Vietnam War, having been modified for electronic countermeasures duty, serving as a "jammer."

With the Skystreak and Skyrocket, their simplified shapes served their research mission well. Combat fighters and strike aircraft, on the other hand, did not lend themselves to such simplicity because, in a way, much more was expected of them – greater load-carrying capacity, more systems, more endurance and range, and more weapons.

At the outset, there was debate about the fuselage design of the Skyknight. EH asked me to design a round fuselage for the fighter. Easier said than done. To meet Navy specifications we had to consider the distance between the body of the aircraft and the ground in case of a flat tire. A round fuselage design didn't allow for enough clearance. But Ed insisted on the round shape. I don't think he considered it an aeronautical commandment. He just preferred round fuselages. It could be done, I explained, if we added five degrees of incidence in the wing (The angle of incidence is the acute angle between the chord of its wings and the longitudinal axis of an aircraft.) This proved correct.

As a weight-saving measure, instead of ejection seats for the crew, we designed a ventral chute just aft of the seats. The aviators egressed by sliding down the chute, backs to the nose of the aircraft, then pulling their D-rings when clear.

The F3D featured a mid-wing design and was powered by a pair of 3,000-pound-thrust Westinghouse J34 turbojets installed in semi-external nacelles.

The Skyknight was referred to as an "old man's airplane" because of its great handling characteristics, its reliability, and its comparatively low performance. It was quite a departure from the research aircraft, but certainly bolstered my education as a design engineer, and consequently, as an artist.

The bat wing F4D Skyray also reflected gains derived from the Lippish data. The fighter's wing geometry (similar to the A4D's delta-shaped wing, but with rounded tips; it had no horizontal tail), enhanced the climbing ability of the aircraft. The F4D broke numerous speed and climb-to-altitude records. Both the Navy and the Marines flew it. One squadron was the Navy's All-Weather Fighter Squadron Three (VFAW-3). It was a large unit assigned to NORAD, the North Atlantic Defense organization. The squadron's aircraft had a rather unique color scheme highlighted by a star-studded dark strip along the top of the fuselage and over the vertical stabilizer. I was drawing a painting of a VFAW-3 F4D one day when Harry Gann came into the office. (Like me, Harry originally came aboard as an engineer at Douglas, but later became a first-rate aviation historian and writer. Harry is also one of the great aerial photographers of our time.) He said, "Bob, has the squadron changed their color from dark black to dark blue?"

"What do you mean," I said, showing Harry the photograph I was working from. "See, the strip along the top is blue."

"Bob, that strip is black, not blue."

I was a little perplexed, but after further study agreed with Harry. This was my vision's "grey-green weakness," a kind of color blindness, revealing itself. I believed the color in the photo was blue, not black. Harry helped me out on that one.

In the middle to late 1950s, Naval Aviation arguably passed through a period of change greater than any in its history. The effective exploitation of these advances enhanced the speed, firepower, versatility, and mobility of Naval sea and air forces. Guns were being replaced by guided missiles, capability to deliver nuclear weapons was increased, aircraft speed jumped from sub to supersonic, and large, angle-deck carriers were coming along. The atmosphere at Douglas was brimming with energy. We seemed to be steeped into a variety of projects almost simultaneously.

• • •

Ed Heinemann used to say, "If the jet engine had been invented before the reciprocating engine, we would not have had reciprocating engines." He could be right. I do know that Ed and most of us in the field believed that, in a very general sense, you built an aircraft "around" the power plant selected to drive it. Comparatively, jets are not only more powerful than recips, they are simpler in design and easier to maintain.

In the case of the twin-engine A3D Skywarrior (later designated the A-3), which we started to work on in 1947, the power its engines could produce was especially critical. At the time, the Douglas company, particularly the El Segundo Division, was developing a reputation as the "General Motors of Aviation." The Skywarrior would prove to be one of its most enduring and, with respect to the Cold War that soon enveloped the major world powers in a lethal competition of armed might, most important creations. Why? Because, although we weren't specifically told about it at the time, we suspected the Skywarrior would have to be able to carry a nuclear weapon on a long-range, deep-strike mission, most likely from a carrier in the Mediterranean, into the far, mountainous recesses of the Soviet Union.

The size of the weapon, carried internally, was not specified to those of us on the design team. Only the basic parameters and requirements were handed down because of the highly classified nature of nuclear weapon technology at that time. Even so, I had a "Q" clearance, which allowed me to become acquainted with some of the classified information related to the atomic bomb.

The Skywarrior became the heaviest aircraft ever designed for routine operations from an aircraft carrier. Originally, it was planned to fly from what was to be a brand-new "super" carrier. The weapon itself weighed 10,000 pounds. The swept-wing bomber had to be able to travel 2,000 miles, execute the attack, then return to the carrier. Gross weight could not exceed 100,000 pounds, according to Navy specifications. New turbojet engines were planned. The pilot would be assisted by a bombardier-navigator next to him and a third crewman-gunner just behind the pilot in the cockpit, along with a scientist to tend to the bomb.

We mounted the wing atop the fuselage, allowing sufficient space in the internal bomb bay for the weapon. Because the wing was shoulder-mounted we designed a narrow-track undercarriage, with the wheels retracting rearward into the fuselage. The engines were installed in individual pods below and forward of the wing. Fuel was stored in tanks in inner sections of the wing and in the fuselage.

Saving weight anywhere we could was critical. Ed Heinemann was running the show and decided that in an emergency, an escape chute for the crew, like that in the F3D Skyknight, would suffice. Ejection seats were fine but heavy. Also, they weren't totally reliable in those days. This decision saved us 3,500 pounds.

Ed was very aware of a high-profile feud between the Navy and Air Force over the long-range strike mission. He feared the super carrier on the drawing boards might be canceled. As a matter of fact, it was, but a similar one came on the line a few years later. Ed figured if we made the A3D light enough, it could operate from the decks of existing, smaller flattops of the Midway class.

We won the competition over the Curtiss and North American companies and turned in a plane with a gross weight of 68,000 pounds, an absolutely remarkable achievement, helped by the development of a lighter-weight nuclear bomb. The challenge we met was immense. Our detractors were stunned when the A3D came in well below 100,000 pounds. The Skywarrior went on to serve in the Navy inventory for nearly 40 years, as a deep-strike bomber from the outset, and later on as an in-flight refueling aircraft, as a photo-reconnaissance plane, and as an electronic-intelligence gatherer, among other missions. The Skywarrior served in the Vietnam and Gulf Wars.

In talking with Ed Heinemann one day he described an idea he had for a "point interceptor," a diminutive aircraft that weighed only 8,500 pounds and was hardly more than a small Skystreak with a pair of guns installed in the wings and a single pilot at the controls. Its mission: launch from the carrier, proceed 100 miles toward the threat, shoot the threat down with its guns, and return to the ship. Ed asked our design group the rhetorical question, "How small and simple an airplane could we design?"

We set out to work on this mini-fighter about the same time the Navy laid out a requirement for a carrier-based attack plane of small dimensions that could carry an atomic weapon, deliver it on a target 400 miles from the flattop, then return to the ship. The Navy figured such an airplane should not exceed 30,000 pounds.

Perhaps it was the exercise with the point interceptor that conditioned us, and especially Heinemann, into thinking we could design the aircraft at one-half that weight, around 15,000 pounds. In some quarters we were ridiculed for even thinking such thoughts. Yet Ed said, "Let's cut the weight in half and see what happens."

One thing about the design process and the weight people was well known in those days. The weight engineers dealt constantly with target figures set forth by the customer. Once they heard 30,000 pounds, they automatically planned the max weight at 29,000 pounds, 1,000 pounds under. They knew full well that aircraft inevitably gained weight as increased capabilities were assigned to the aircraft, often quite soon after it reached the fleet. Increased capabilities imposed on the plane translated to more hardware somewhere on the aircraft, and more hardware meant more weight. The 1,000-pound "fudge" factor was built in to compensate for the inevitable.

History proved that if we added a 100-pound system to a plane, we were really adding 600 pounds – to accommodate the extra 100 pounds. More wing size might be required to handle the 100 pounds, plus the capacity for more fuel might have to be increased. A kind of domino effect.

Yet here was Ed Heinemann telling us to shoot for half of the anticipated weight of 30,000 pounds! "A 15,000 pound attack bomber?" some said, "who are you kidding?"

But we weren't kidding.

I discovered early on in this effort that if we held the wing span to twenty-seven and a half feet (a factor the Navy readily knew), two of these airplanes could pass each other on the hangar deck of an aircraft without folding the wings. And if a wing-folding mechanism wasn't needed we could save precious pounds. Plus, the maneuverability in the crowded confines of a carrier hangar deck was a huge plus in the eyes of the Navy.

With a wing span of only twenty-seven and one-half feet, we had trouble finding enough space to contain the retractable landing gear. I knew I could create more depth inside the wing itself by keeping the same percentage thickness and adding area to the wing. Since Ed didn't like broken trailing edges, we decided to draw a straight line from wing tip to wing tip. I liked the design both from the engineering aspect (which provided the space needed for the landing gear) and aesthetically, as an artist. I was, however, concerned, since our aspect ratio was now less than four. Heinemann also liked the design and, despite the warnings from Aero, made the historic decision to press forward until someone could prove it wouldn't work. Thus was born the A4D (later the A-4) delta wing, an achievement that helped make the Skyhawk one of the great warplanes in history.

Ed Heinemann fought a constant battle against excess weight in aircraft. Lighter was better, and we all agreed with him and worked to keep the planes as light as possible, knowing the enhanced performance of the aircraft would be worth it. And it was, because the A-4 Skyhawk became one of Douglas' all-time winners.

In all modesty, of all the aircraft I worked on over the years, the A-4 bears more of my imprint than any other airplane. Its maiden sortie took place in June 1954 with the great Douglas experimental test pilot, Bob Rahn, at the controls.

As we increased the flight parameters we did encounter a variety of problems, but we countered the flaws as they came along.

The A4D was a diminutive airplane, but it could deliver a nuclear bomb just as well as the Skywarrior, although it transported the weapon externally on the centerline station. The A4D had several popular nicknames, including Heinemann's Hot Rod, Tinker Toy, Scooter, and Bantam Bomber.

Two thousand nine hundred and sixty (2,960) A-4s, in a multitude of configurations, were built through the years. The Skyhawk was a war horse in the Vietnam War. It was acquired by many allied countries. And at this writing, nearly 40 years after we began working on the plane, the two-seat version is used to train strike/fighter pilots in the Navy.

Incidentally, the last Skyhawk was an A-4M delivered to the Marines in 1979. Before the ceremony planned for the event, Harry Gann came into the office with a model of this plane he had had the modeling shop at Douglas spiff up with a commemorative color scheme. I made some suggestions and doctored up the design quite differently, but Harry liked the result. I trimmed the upper nose and top fuselage in light blue, included the Blue Angel emblem on the side below the cockpit, then ran a strip of flags along the sides of the fuselage representing the various nations that operated the Skyhawk. The Marines liked it so much they left the color scheme intact for some time after they operated the aircraft. It was a showpiece wherever it went.

• • •

When I started working at Douglas, my non-technical drawings, such as the one of the BT-1 which I produced for Ed Heinemann to use during a presentation to the Navy, were ancillary projects not required by my job description. I was never ordered to produce these. I did them because I was asked and because my love of drawing was as strong then as it was later in my life.

I never had any formal instruction or training in art. My approaches to color and technique were destined to change significantly, however, after separate encounters with two very talented individuals.

When I started producing drawings for Douglas, I was introduced to an illustrator named Bob Poole. He had a great sense of humor, and we hit it off right away. Bob taught me some early tricks about the use of basic colors (red, blue, and yellow) by showing me how to blend and "grey down" vivid colors. He also taught me that by blending colors, I could add motion to an aircraft and add subtlety to harsh lines.

A significant revelation to me, the moment when "I saw the light," so to speak, came when I discovered the value of tempera. Tempera is the opaque form of watercolor and does wonders enhancing the primary impression of a painting when executed with transparent watercolor. Used properly, tempera helps balance a picture and accentuates distance between the subject and the background.

Bob Poole loved airplanes, too. We moonlighted to earn extra money by drawing inboard profiles or illustrating the covers and pages of aviation publications. We worked together on these jobs, and were both happy to have the extra income. Often, while the wives went shopping for the day, Bob and I packed our gear, which included a flask of bourbon, and headed to the San Gabriel mountains to paint. He and his wife eventually moved to Oregon, but we stayed in touch and remained lifelong friends until his death in 1997.

As my engineering efforts continued, the requests for drawings, and eventually, paintings, increased. In fact, if a request for a picture came in while I was in the middle of a detailed engineering problem, the interruption, at times, was a nuisance. As the requests for paintings increased, I was getting more and more exposure as an aviation artist. Since the engineering work was highly classified – done "behind closed doors" –

and the art was becoming more visible, people began to view me mainly as an artist.

Finding Arthur Beaumont sitting on that bench painting the Skystreak in 1947 was one of the luckiest days of my career. It was Beaumont who taught me composition, color balance, and how to look at a subject, and translate the visual image to paper or canvas.

Beaumont also taught me discipline. He put our student group through disciplinary exercises on alternate Saturdays of the month in the Long Beach/San Pedro Harbor area. During these seminars we sketched in the morning, held discussions on art over brown bag lunches at noon, then painted in the afternoon.

Attention to detail was mandatory. Beaumont used to say, "There are no straight lines on ships. Hulls are curved." He instructed us to stare at a subject, form it in our mind for a minute or so, then turn our backs to the subject and sketch it. We repeated this practice, increasing the time to two minutes, then three, then four. When we reached the five minute point, we realized we weren't seeing much.

Eventually this exercise taught me how critical it is to observe and remember detail. Soon I was able to turn my back and duplicate what I had seen. Occasionally, Douglas sent me on field trips where cameras weren't allowed. I had to sketch from memory. Beaumont's exercises proved invaluable.

Understanding light and its effects is obviously critical to an artist. With Beaumont, after sketching in the morning, we took up watercolors in the afternoon. For instance, as the descending sun caught the side of a rusty tanker, it created a startling bright copper tone. We learned that if we didn't try to emulate that color on paper within 30 minutes, the light would be lost, and the rich copper tone would quickly change to a dingy, lifeless brown.

Beaumont liked to talk about the old masters, pointing out their strengths and their greatness. He would take a picture by one of the old masters, lay a piece of tissue over it, then shade in the dark areas, to demonstrate the pattern the artist had created in designing the overall composition of his work. He did the same with the lighter areas, shading in those sections on the tissue paper, then exhibiting the resulting design.

He enhanced harbor scenes with little Vs we came to call "Beaumont sea gulls." The Vs actually resembled birds, and were effective in carrying the viewer's eyes around a painting. Beaumont emphasized it wasn't necessary to reproduce an exact replica of a scene as long as the end result achieved dramatic impact. His rather flamboyant style and use of bright colors depicting ships certainly vividly achieved this.

Even though it wasn't necessary to portray every rivet in the aircraft, I had to be extremely accurate in my renditions at Douglas, because these aircraft were our products. They had to be depicted honestly and realistically, especially when painted as proposals for prospective customers. Beaumont didn't agree with this emphasis on finite accuracy. He knew Ed Heinemann and often chided Ed about letting me have more freedom, with respect to the art I produced for Douglas.

Years later, Beaumont was quoted as saying of my work, "Poor be the student who does not exceed his teacher, and that, most assuredly, R.G. has done." This is one of the greatest compliments I ever received, but I must humbly admit I will always consider Beaumont the master.

Soon after the war, Betty and I had saved enough to build a home in the rural community of Palos Verdes Estates, which at the time was considered horse country and an ideal place to raise a family. It was also conveniently close to the San Pedro Bay/Long Beach area where I liked spending occasional Saturdays painting ships and boats and other old relics.

It was during my tenure with Beaumont that I started to branch out to other subjects and medium. Although I began painting watercolors of boats and ships around San Pedro Harbor, I soon decided to try oils (around 1952). I found oils much more forgiving, since I could change or paint over something I wasn't satisfied with.

I don't know how a psychologist would analyze me, but I was always fascinated by old relics. Maybe it had something to do with my love of history. With oils, I expanded my subjects from ships and boats to old shacks and barns, abandoned gold mines, and other scenes of the old West.

As time went on and business improved, Douglas enhanced its favorable reputation because of its remarkable aircraft production during the 1950s and early 1960s. I believe all of us in those early years enjoyed the individuality of participating in the process. There were fewer of us, so the sense of teamwork was always inherent. There was meaningful interplay between seniors and subordinates as we all strived toward a common goal, producing the best possible bomber, attack, or transport plane on the market. There was considerable give and take, but those days were rapidly disappearing.

The size of the work force had multiplied. Individual decisions gave way to committee decisions. Individual efforts seemed to fade in importance to the overall product. One meeting would spawn a succession of meetings, and the decision making process became more and more prolonged and complicated.

Also during this transition, calculators were taking the place of slide rules, and the advent of computers was changing every phase of the engineering process. I started developing a rather tainted view of committee actions and the changing times. Engineering just wasn't as much fun anymore, and I realized that engineering, as I knew it, was reaching the end of an era.

Even so, I hasten to add I was honored with an affirmation of our early contributions to the aircraft industry. I was presented an award from Leo Devlin, then Chief Engineer at Douglas, commemorating my "Outstanding Contributions to the Science of Aeronautics in the Design, Configuration and Arrangement of Combat Aircraft." EH used to say of our early design group, "We were making history with these airplanes, but were too busy having fun to know it." Even though the times had changed, I was proud to have been a part of this effort.

While interest in my engineering duties was decreasing, the desire to paint airplanes grew. The company recognized the value of my paintings as a growing asset for public relations and promotional purposes. I was producing a countless number of drawings and paintings for Douglas, which the company used for lithographs, calendars, proposals, and various publications – all for promoting the company's wares.

Buddy Gilman, who was in charge of customer relations and a good friend, requested paintings for military magazines, company publications, or prospective and existing customers, on a regular basis. I kept busy with a blossoming backlog of requests.

I also executed cover art for aviation publications such as Approach (Naval Aviation's safety magazine), Naval Aviation News (the official voice of Naval Aviation), and U.S. Naval Institute Proceedings (a professional journal), along with several other publications. It made sense to contribute to these magazines, because they reached the people who flew and maintained the aircraft, plus those in industry who had an acute interest in the subject.

At no cost to the government, and usually as a result of a friendly request from the Navy, I painted Douglas aircraft and other military aviation and combat scenes for these periodicals. Looking back, I am happy to have produced several dozen covers for these pubs over the years. Painting thus became my primary occupation at Douglas.

I was most fortunate in having Norma Bert assigned to me. She was a capable and loyal assistant who came on board in 1960. She helped me keep track of the increasing number of paintings and drawings in my inventory, and handled the routine paperwork, which I have always found tedious and avoided whenever possible. She also acted as liaison, handling the growing correspondence and other related issues that arose on a daily basis. Basically, she made my life much easier, so I was free to concentrate on my art.

In 1979, staff artist Mike Machat was assigned to us to help in the production of gold-foil etchings commemorating the roll-out of the last of the A-4 Skyhawks built by Douglas. Mike's enthusiasm for art was terrific, and I was pleased to help him all I could. He often asked me to examine his art work, and I pointed out a shortcoming here and there, which Mike sincerely appreciated. He had a sailplane, and took me, Betty, my daughter and her three children flying one day, which was great fun. Mike also worked on VIP calendars and related tasks.

It wasn't long before I was painting Douglas' commercial as well as military aircraft. The DC-9, for example, was a huge success. Many airlines bought the twin-jet airliner, and I painted it in the color schemes of the various airlines which operated it. As the request for paintings for commercial customers increased, our little operation was likened to a satellite public relations office for the company.

An important milestone took place when Douglas merged with the McDonnell Corporation in 1967, forming the McDonnell Douglas Corporation. I worked for Douglas and McDonnell Douglas from 1936 to 1982, when I retired. The Monday following my retirement, I returned to the company as an outside contractor, maintaining the spacious office, drafting tables, and ideal studio conditions the company had so generously provided me for years. I remained in that capacity until fully retiring in 1991.

The fall of the iron curtain and relative peace in the world led to the downsizing of the U.S. military in the late 1980s. The inevitable dismantling of huge elements of the aviation industry followed. One significant development: McDonnell Douglas was acquired by the Boeing Company in 1997.

• • •

On occasion I was among small groups of the engineering staff who visited air bases and aircraft carriers to witness first-hand and up close how the Navy was operating its Douglas aircraft. It was quite amazing, and certainly enlightening, to see our products at work, especially in the tough and occasionally hazardous environment of the flight deck on aircraft carriers.

My first trip of note took place in August, 1944. Along with a group of four other engineers from Douglas, I was sent to observe aircraft during carrier operations under combat conditions. The USS Ticonderoga, then en route down the eastern seaboard, picked us up in Norfolk, Virginia. In the next week we traveled through the Panama Canal, where we observed nearly 700 takeoffs and landings performed both day and night. We disembarked in San Diego, after which the Ticonderoga continued west to join the war in the Pacific. We came away from this journey with many new ideas for future military aircraft designs. Incidentally, it was on this trip I met a young Naval Aviator named Zeke Cormier. He later became a double ace and personified the warrior spirit of our flyers.

In May, 1957, I was sent to the carrier, USS Bon Homme Richard, to study carrier operations, another enlightening experience. But the real highlight of my life came a decade later and was embodied in two separate trips to the war zone in Southeast Asia. I spent a month there in 1968 and another month in 1969 as a combat artist for the Navy.

I had floated the idea to my superiors about going to Vietnam where the fighting had already intensified. What better way to further enhance the image of the organization than to show McDonnell Douglas aircraft in action? The Navy agreed to let me go. It wanted me to capture the war first-hand by producing a collection of art depicting our Navy in action, not just McDonnell Douglas aircraft. Buddy Gilman negotiated the arrangements and saw to it that I was afforded a rank equal to a Navy captain in order to facilitate travel and observation anywhere I wanted to go. I experienced carrier operations in the blue waters of Yankee Station in the Gulf of Tonkin; riverine patrols along the muddy brown water of the Mekong Delta; search and rescue operations in Huey helicopters; and OV-10 Bronco attack duty. I also witnessed the daily suffering of the South Vietnamese people. I filled numerous sketchbooks with disturbing and unforgettable impressions.

I was in my mid-50s at the time, twice the age of most of the kids I rode with, and certainly not physically as capable. Yet I kept up with them, fueled by the adrenaline that shot through me every time the going got rough or I found myself in harm's way.

One of the unfortunate and unusual aspects of the Vietnam conflict was that more often than not, it was difficult to tell whether we were facing friend or foe. Several times while observing ground operations, we found ourselves in a dangerous situation. Helicopters would swoop down to rescue us, allowing just enough time to jump on the landing bar and pull ourselves inside while dangling in mid air and ascending to our escape. At my age, this was quite a physical challenge. Yet, on such occasions, I could literally feel a sudden burst of added energy giving me the strength I needed.

One time the Viet Cong were suspected of meeting in an underground tunnel they had devised. We were tasked with breaking up the meeting and destroying the tunnel. The helicopter pilot circled around and around until we saw a group of boats tied up beneath us. The pilot surmised the meeting was taking place under the boats. He circled a little longer, deciding indeed it was. He told the side gunner to shoot up the boats. It was a peculiar situation because, as with so many of the conflicts in that war, success and failure were hard to determine. Unlike most wars, there were very few lines of demarcation. Dense jungle and foliage camouflaged enemy activities, enemies were often mistaken for friends and vice versa, and the conflicts were rarely defined with wins and losses. We shot up the boats but never learned if we broke up a meeting.

Riding in the back seat of an OV-10 Bronco, a light attack plane, was exciting. I flew with the famed Black Ponies of Light Attack Squadron Four (VAL-4). In order to suppress ground fire as we patrolled an area near the South Vietmese/Cambodian border, we were equipped with pods containing Zuni rockets and 7.62 caliber machine guns. While airborne we received an urgent transmission from a contingent of ground troops surrounded by Viet Cong. They needed help. Could we come? My pilot said, "We're on the way," and we were rapidly vectored toward the site in company with our wingman in another OV-10. A few moments later, we were over the patrol, which was cloaked by jungle and darkness. One of them radioed directions where they thought the enemy was and where they wanted our rockets to go.

Our Black Ponies went to work, climbing, diving, firing rockets, then repositioning for several more runs. I was really pumped, pulling g's in the OV-10 and wheeling aggressively through the sky. I was especially exhilarated when tracer fire burst from out of the black jungle up toward us. I was captivated by the brilliance and length of the plumes of flame emanating from our rockets, noting the plumes were twice as long as the rocket itself. Watching the tracers, I couldn't help drawing mental pictures in my mind's eye. How was I going to depict this action in a painting?

Fortunately, we weren't hit, and after three more attacks we returned to base. It wasn't until I climbed out of the aircraft and stepped onto to mother earth that I realized how close we had come to being hit by the ground fire. It occurred to me that in between those tracers aimed at our OV-10 were a half-dozen live rounds of ammo. There I was, thinking how to effectively portray the action in art, rather than properly fearing it.

On another occasion, I was cleared to travel with a crew on a riverine patrol boat in the Delta of South Vietnam, an unnerving experience, to be sure. It was night, and you didn't know who was who, but you had a real sense the enemy was out there watching us, while the VC probably thought we were watching them. We had heard that the Viet Cong were moving supplies to their troops, and we were sent to stop them. We started to move. A crewman handed me a M-16 rifle. "Just in case," he said. I was unfamiliar with the weapon, but was sufficiently knowledgeable to chamber a round.

Unbeknownst to us, a Republic of Korea gun battery nearby, but inland from us, had received the same information and was firing its cannons at the VC. We were told to be very quiet as the boat moved slowly along the shallow waters of the Delta. We got word from friendly villagers that some sort of fire fight was impending. There was a whistling sound in the night, followed by a boom. There were explosions along the bank of the river. These were mortars, or some kind of cannon fire.

Something brushed the side of the boat. I asked one of the four crewmen on board about this sound. "Shrapnel hitting the boat," he said.

Just then, the lieutenant who commanded the vessel said, "Let's get the hell out of here!" not knowing where the fire power was coming from, but acutely aware we were well within its range. We departed the area in a hurry.

I never did fire the M-16 that night, although I derived satisfaction from being told later by the lieutenant that my "armed" presence increased the firepower of the patrol boat by 20 percent!

My times aboard ships were probably the most influential, with respect to my combat art. I asked my Navy escorts if I could go aboard one of the destroyers accompanying the carrier, USS Midway, in order to view flight operations of the flattop from a distance. Midway was on Yankee Station located off the North Vietnamese coast. It was the staging area from which air strikes were launched against the North. I got the OK, jumped aboard a helicopter, and away we went.

The destroyer was traveling at a pretty good clip, and since the water was rough, a crewman said, "We can't land on the tin can due to the high seas, so we're going to lower you down by the hoist."

I donned a harness and was attached to the hoist cable, feeling a bit uneasy, although I had the fullest confidence in the crew.

"Sit on the edge of the hatch," I was told. I obeyed, beginning to sense there was a little more to this adventure than I anticipated, as my legs dangled out the opening. We were 100 feet above the surface, about ten stories high.

"We'll signal you when we're going to lower you," said the crewman. I was looking down at the destroyer and the broiling whitecaps when the crewman tapped me on the shoulder and gave me a kind of shove. Suddenly, I was out there with nothing underneath me but the destroyer and the deep blue sea. My adrenaline was really flowing as I descended in mid-air toward the waiting ship.

I landed safely, and ultimately was able to enjoy a new perspective of carrier operations. On the flattop, the decibel level of launching jets is ear-shattering. From my vantage point on the destroyer, it was like watching a silent movie.

From my experience on the nuclear-powered carrier, USS Enterprise, I was able to reconstruct one of the more amazing feats of airmanship by our Navy flyers, called "wet-wing." On several occasions, the A-3 Skywarrior, at this point in its long history now functioning as an in-flight refueling aircraft, refueled a damaged A-4 Skyhawk as it led the smaller aircraft back to the ship following a combat mission. The A-4 "plugged" into the A-3's refueling hose, which extended from the rear fuselage of the Skywarrior. The Skyhawk, hit by enemy fire in its fuel-laden wing, was losing fuel as it streamed from a hole in the wing, but the A-3 continuously replenished it. The Skywarrior led the Skyhawk down the glide slope, positioning the A-4 as close to the ship as possible before the aircraft disengaged from each other. The A-3 waved off, and the A-4 continued to an arrested landing. Teamwork personified!

During my two trips to Vietnam, I visited the aircraft carriers Midway, Kitty Hawk, Constellation, and Enterprise, in addition to many of the support ships. I am ever thankful for the opportunity to see first-hand what our military was up against in this bizarre, tragic war. I never shied away from being in a combat zone, because it was the only way to document the way it really was. In the process, I verified a feeling I had been harboring for some time: that many of the military decisions were being made in Washington and not on the front lines. I have often felt the outcome of this war might have been a swift victory for us rather than the slow defeat it became, had our military been given a free hand to run operations.

During my career, I was lucky enough to be invited to participate in two more military operations and to depict them through art. In April 1983, I watched Fleet Ex 83, a joint effort with the Canadians, in the Aleutian Island area, where the various units practiced military maneuvers under extreme weather conditions. Days could be warm and sunny, or brutally cold, with temperatures 45 degrees below zero due to the wind factor. The temperature swing, as it was explained to me, is caused by the warm Japanese current meeting the frigid Arctic air at the Pacific rim. The catch phrase in the area was, "If you don't like the temperature now, wait an hour."

Our transport made a hair-raising landing at Adak, Alaska, during a storm. The wind was fierce, and sleet was blowing horizontally, a sight I had never seen before. In the two weeks I was there, the temperature was usually well below freezing, making it difficult for this old vet, now nearly 70 years old, to commit much to my sketch pad. I had to rely on snapping photos, which I later translated to sketches and paintings. I rode on Canadian frigates, U.S. Coast Guard cutters, and the carriers, Midway and Coral Sea. However, some operations were canceled due to the severe weather.

Incidentally, on my last day there, the sun came out and reflected off the snow everywhere. It was a beautiful sight.

The following year the Navy invited me to visit operations on the island Diego Garcia, in the Indian Ocean, and at Subic Bay in the Philippines. Diego Garcia is the only base the Navy and Air Force operated in the Indian Ocean. Subic Bay is absolutely beautiful. I had a difficult time selecting the sketches I wanted to paint because there were so many compelling and noteworthy scenes there.

This "final" tour was memorable, and was a nice way to round out my travels as a combat artist. It sure was a lot easier to sketch on Diego Garcia or at Subic Bay, compared to the cold and bleak Aleutian area.

My brief exposure to duty with the troops reinforced in me a passion and respect I have always felt for our warriors, especially those in the U.S. Navy and Marine Corps. How lucky we are in this country to have people like these, who make such magnificent and often unrecognized sacrifices in our behalf.

In my later years, when I received some very prestigious honors from the Navy, I never was able to properly express the unbounded gratitude I felt, and still feel, for having been associated with such exemplary Americans.

• • •

As I enter the final chapters of my life, I feel a twinge of guilt for having had so much fun. I'm not a complicated man, and it has never taken much in the way of material things to make me happy. Most of my pleasures have come from my family, my career, my hobbies, my books, and my friends. The wonderful experiences and opportunities that came my way were frosting on the cake.

Looking back on my life, I derive great satisfaction from having participated in the conceptual and configuration phase of virtually every tactical military airplane built by the Douglas Aircraft Company in its heyday. The "Sky" series of aircraft were especially important to our Naval and Marine forces during war and peace. My work has been recognized by numerous awards and presentations, but I have always been surprised and moved by such occasions.

The most prestigious and overwhelming of these awards took place May 8, 1973. McDonnell Douglas was delivering its first C-9 Skytrain II transport to the Navy at a ceremony in Long Beach, California. Vice Admiral Bill Houser, Deputy Chief of Naval Operations for Air Warfare, was on hand for the occasion. Since I was trying to meet a deadline, I hadn't planned to attend the festivities. However, my assistant, who was in on the secret, tricked me into going out to the flight line where everyone had gathered. Admiral Houser was at the podium, and suddenly, to my utter surprise, called me forward. He presented me the most coveted citation of my career. I was designated an Honorary Navy Aviator, only the tenth individual, at that point in time, to be so honored. I had joined the ranks of such company as Admiral Hyman Rickover, father of the nuclear ship Navy, and Senator John Warner, former Secretary of the Navy. Bob Hope became Honorary Naval Aviator No. 19 for his decades of service to the troops abroad, and the great Jimmie Doolittle was also named to the list later on.

I was still in shock when Admiral Houser asked me to say a few words. All I could muster was a clumsy "thank you" in response. I have relived that moment many times. I only wish I had been prepared to more fully express my appreciation and gratitude.

I am deeply grateful for the opportunities I have had to explore new avenues. I count among my most thrilling experiences a rear seat ride with the Navy's precision flying team, the Blue Angels. I rode in their TA-4 Skyhawk after I was designated an honorary Blue Angel 1979. The Blues are a superb group of professionals, and wonderful representatives of Naval Aviation.

I have always had an insatiable thirst to expand my knowledge and experiences and to open new doors. Along with my career as an aviation and combat artist, I have explored, studied, and experimented with many other mediums and venues of art. I have painted barns and shacks, abandoned mines, Indians, and various scenes from the old west. I have studied the drawing of figures and nudes. For a time, I sculpted the names of family and friends in Egyptian hieroglyphics. I also went through a phase studying a process of etching. I have tried most every medium, including watercolor, tempera, acrylic, oils, charcoal, pastel, pencil, and pen. At one point I built my own lapidary shop and learned to cut and polish stones and rocks. These I gathered from local beaches and from annual driving vacations through the western states. From these I made pieces of jewelry for Betty and managed to chisel scores of Indian arrowheads for myself.

Along with my lifelong love of the outdoors, I liked working with my hands, and did most of the construction and landscaping around our homes. In our first home I landscaped the front and back yards, then built a fence around the perimeter. We used to pile the kids into our Studebaker and take them a mile up the road to the canyons and gullies which were full of flagstone, or what is commonly known nowadays as Palos Verdes stone. With hammer and crowbar we chiseled out large chunks of stone and hauled them home, where I laid an entire patio, complete with planters and built-in barbecue.

We stayed in that home until the children were grown. Rick graduated valedictorian of his class and attended the University of California at Berkley on a scholarship. Sharlyn worked at Space Technology Laboratories, decoding launch data while attending classes at UCLA. Both children married and blessed Betty and me with eight beautiful grandchildren and nine great-grandchildren.

After the children left home we bought our second house in Rolling Hills Estates which sat on a steep knoll with a spectacular panoramic view of the city and San Pedro Harbor. I had to design a drainage system in order to keep the rear hill from washing down onto the house when it rained. I installed a sprinkler system and terraced the slopes with railroad ties to retain the wet soil and groundcover.

I mentioned these projects only to express the enjoyment I had in designing and engineering solutions to our needs, and working with my hands.

I never lost interest in history, especially the Civil War. Writing this book with Zip, he reminded me of the time in the 1970s, while on a business trip to Washington D.C., that he drove me to the Gettysburg battlefields in Pennsylvania. We rented one of those audio programs and listened to a description of the various troop emplacements and battle sites as we drove through the fields. To Zip's amazement, I had studied the battle so thoroughly, I could actually identify an area before we got there. Beaumont's insistence on "attention to detail," I suppose.

I always looked forward to my annual one-week camping trip with "the boys." Every year, Wilbur "Bill" Bettis (Navy pilot), Al "Ozzie" Oseguera, (Marine fighter/attack pilot), retired Brigadier General Jay "Hub" Hubbard (Marine fighter/attack pilot), and usually one or two newcomers (including my son, Rick, who joined us one year), would pack our gear and head north to "gold" country. We hiked, dug, and panned for gold during the day. But the real fun occurred at night by the campfire, toasting and roasting, and trying to outdo each other with war stories and jokes.

This all started in 1970 when Harry Gann and his wife, Deloris, were invited by Blue Angels Dick Schram and Skip Olmstead to dinner at a restaurant owned by Bill Bettis, eventually known as the very popular Nieuport 17. Harry noticed one of my paintings over the bar and said he knew the artist, yours truly. Bill called me to talk about the painting, and this ignited a friendship between us that expanded to Ozzie and Hub and has lasted all these years.

We weren't really roughing it on those camping trips. Bill's Nieuport 17 supplied us with gourmet food for the week, and Jay's wife Dorla always sent along her famous potato salad. We also gathered several times a year at Nieuport 17, and for 27 years in a row, attended the annual dinner that Bill hosted for the Blue Angels during their performance at nearby El Toro. That tradition sadly ended this year (1998) with the planned closing of MCAS El Toro.

A descendant who developed my love of art and airplanes is Sharlyn's son, Steve Tack. Where I loved designing aircraft, Steve loves to fly them. I am proud of him, and flattered that he is a student of my teaching. I am a harsh critic, but I must say that over the past few years, he has joined the ranks of some of the finer young aviation artists of today.

From the time Steve could walk, he would point to airplanes, asking, "What kind, Pappy?" By the time he was five he could identify most of them. His love of aviation has never abated, and his thirst for knowledge and artistic advice continues today.

When asked, "What is the key to becoming a successful artist?," my answer is simple: there are no secrets and no shortcuts. Aspiring artists want to know how to draw and paint, but very few want to take the time to learn. While working with Arthur Beaumont on those alternate Saturdays, I always had the feeling I was getting more out of his class than the other students. I literally hung on his every word, because I truly wanted to improve my abilities.

I advise aspiring artists that the key to success is to refrain from ever being satisfied with your work. Never stop rehearsing your craft. Every painting is another step in an endless learning curve. Achievement comes from hard work, discipline, and a constant program of practice and learning.

The most valuable lesson I learned from Beaumont was discipline, and to treat every painting as if it were a problem to be solved. The three key elements in my approach to painting were: accuracy, planning, and the power of suggestion.

Accuracy requires study and thorough knowledge of your subject. Generally, more than 50 percent of the time I invested in a painting went into research. If I was painting a combat scene, for instance, I studied the history of the battle, and I viewed aircraft and relative subjects from all angles, sometimes even building a scale model of the aircraft or ships I wanted to portray. (When working from a scale model, be aware that various parts of an airplane often change shape and configuration during flight.)

Accumulate a "morgue." I started collecting research material early on in my career. My morgue was comprised of photographs, drawings, and newspaper and magazine articles that profiled virtually every aircraft known to man. Additionally, I kept other materials, including scores of photographs of cloud formations. I collected paint chips or samples from many aircraft to maintain accuracy in color. Whenever I had questions of accuracy I couldn't verify from my own inventory, I called upon my colleague Harry Gann, also an engineer, who became an aerial photographer and Douglas historian.

As to planning a picture, my approach usually entailed making several sketches of ideas for the scene I wanted to create before deciding on the final composition. Adherence to fundamentals is a must. Planning a scene before touching brush to canvas saves problems later. Create the background first, knowing beforehand where you intend to place the aircraft, which should be the last phase of your painting. It often took me three or four days just to put a background together. I took aircraft models and sketched them from different vantage points before deciding how to depict them on canvas. I liked to put an airplane in a picture, not on it. If I had any gift at all, it was the ability to convey through my paintings, as a pilot once told me, "exactly what it's like when you're up there."

Learn how to use the power of suggestion. My criticism of much of aviation art today is that many artists feel they must paint every rivet on an aircraft, or every line on a ship. It often appears as though some artists cut their aircraft from a photograph and paste it on the background. I try to convey a sense of reality, atmosphere, and energy. I am usually more scientific than theoretical. Yet, if you examine my paintings up close, you will note that much of my brush work is rather loose. Stand back and you will see that the overall effect is somewhat like a photograph. It has long been my theory that the eye and the brain do most of the work, connecting the dots and lines. In other words, you don't have to include every detail, just a suggestion of detail.

I had a distinct advantage in painting aircraft because of my engineering work and knowledge of airplanes. I developed a thorough understanding of the innermost construction and functions of an airplane's components. The same holds true for any subject matter. For instance, if you want to draw figures or nudes, learn the structure of the human body first. Before I ever attempted to paint a nude, I studied the structure of muscles and bones in the human body. I drew hands, arms, feet, legs, faces, and torsos, sketching them from several angles and in a multitude of positions. I am convinced if you gain knowledge of the inner workings of your subject, you can literally give it life.

Know your elements, clouds and water, for example. I believe that Charles Evers is a master of painting water. It would be beneficial to study his works if you intend to depict an ocean scene. In other words, study the works of the artists you admire, or whose style you want to emulate.

Years ago, a very good friend, Nan McCandliss, who worked in the library at Douglas, knew I was an admirer of Frank Wooten, the versatile and talented English artist. She collected photographs and reproductions of his work and saved them for me. I not only enjoyed his works, I studied his techniques.

I have always loved the beauty of cloud formations, whether they seem to be brooding, tranquil, or just a miracle of patterns across the sky. My renditions of clouds have been interpreted by critics as a reflection of my mood at the time, or an analysis of what I might have been thinking while painting a scene. It's a popular practice for critics to discuss theory and analysis nowadays, but as for cloud formations, I read nothing more into them beyond the fact they can be fascinating, beautiful, or simply pleasing to my eye. I just like to paint clouds. I believe it was Freud who said, "Sometimes a cigar is just a cigar."

There are a couple of cliches that apply to painting, and I ascribe to both. "Build your stage and put the actors in it," and "Put the subject matter in the picture, not on it." Some artists only see an airplane as a mechanical object. As a result, their depiction of them are mechanical, stilted portraits of aircraft rather than a picture with character, motion, or some measure of dramatic quality.

Grandson Steve wrote in Aviation Illustrated magazine (January 1996) that I was born with "red/green color weak" vision. This is true. I have trouble seeing these colors as others do. I didn't realize this early on, but when I became aware of it, I learned to compensate for the problem by training myself to discern subtleties in shade and value variations. Steve theorized this deficiency could be the origin of my so-called "grayed palette." He believes this is the secret to my sense of realism. Could be.

I have never counted all the paintings I have done. Those on flying and nautical subjects, including the combat art, number well over 1,500. I am proud and flattered that my works are on exhibit in museums and military facilities around the world.

Late in 1990, I suffered an attack of the puzzling virus known as Guillain-Barre', commonly referred to as the "French Polio," since its symptoms so closely resemble polio. I refer to this as the period in my life when the roof fell in. Within months, I was forced to retire and leave the job I had enjoyed for so many years.

Betty and I had put our house on the market so we could move to the desert, where I thought she would be better off due to her arthritic condition. Happily, the house sold the day after I came home from the hospital. Weeks of therapy followed as I tried to regain use of my limbs.

Eventually, I retrained myself to hold a paint brush, but was never able to paint again without severe limitations. Instead, I began a new phase by drawing American Indians, a subject and culture that has interested me since boyhood.

Subsequently, in 1995 I was diagnosed with a rare form of Parkinson's disease. It has further limited my mobility, but has not stopped Betty and me from enjoying life in our beautiful home overlooking a golf course in Rancho Mirage, California.

Sharlyn is handling my collection of art. She keeps me busy signing prints and lithographs. I walk a mile every day with assistance for my balance from my devoted caretaker, Ramon Reyes, and his wife, Patricia.

Most of all, Betty and I are enjoying our grandchildren and our great grandchildren as they weave the tapestries of their lives.

If given the opportunity to rewrite the course of my life, I would change but one pathway. I would have liked to serve my country on the front lines. I believe this is one of the reasons serving the Navy as a combat artist means so very much to me.

# HIS ART

## the early years

"Sioux Indian on a Horse," my first published picture, appeared in "Aunt Elsie's Column" in the Oakland Tribune when I was 13 years old.

ABOVE: Early oil painted in 1929 depicts a British DeHavilland biplane.

TOP RIGHT: In this early watercolor a British Sopwith biplane attacks the German Zeppelin L-39 during World War I action.

RIGHT: Pencil drawing of a German Albatross fighter, done in 1933.

This image of the BT-1 is the first official picture I drew for Jack Northrop. He and Ed Heinemann took it to Washington to show to the Navy. Tommy Stockbridge, an old time actor who was in charge of files at the company, had given me a can of graphite to use for the background. This "discovery" influenced the dark shading effect of my future works.

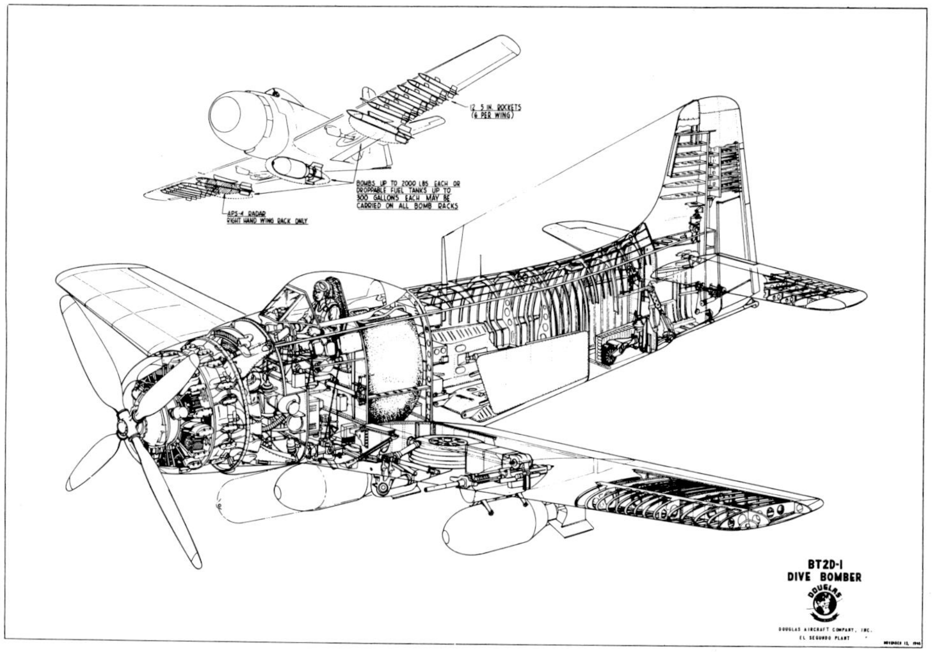


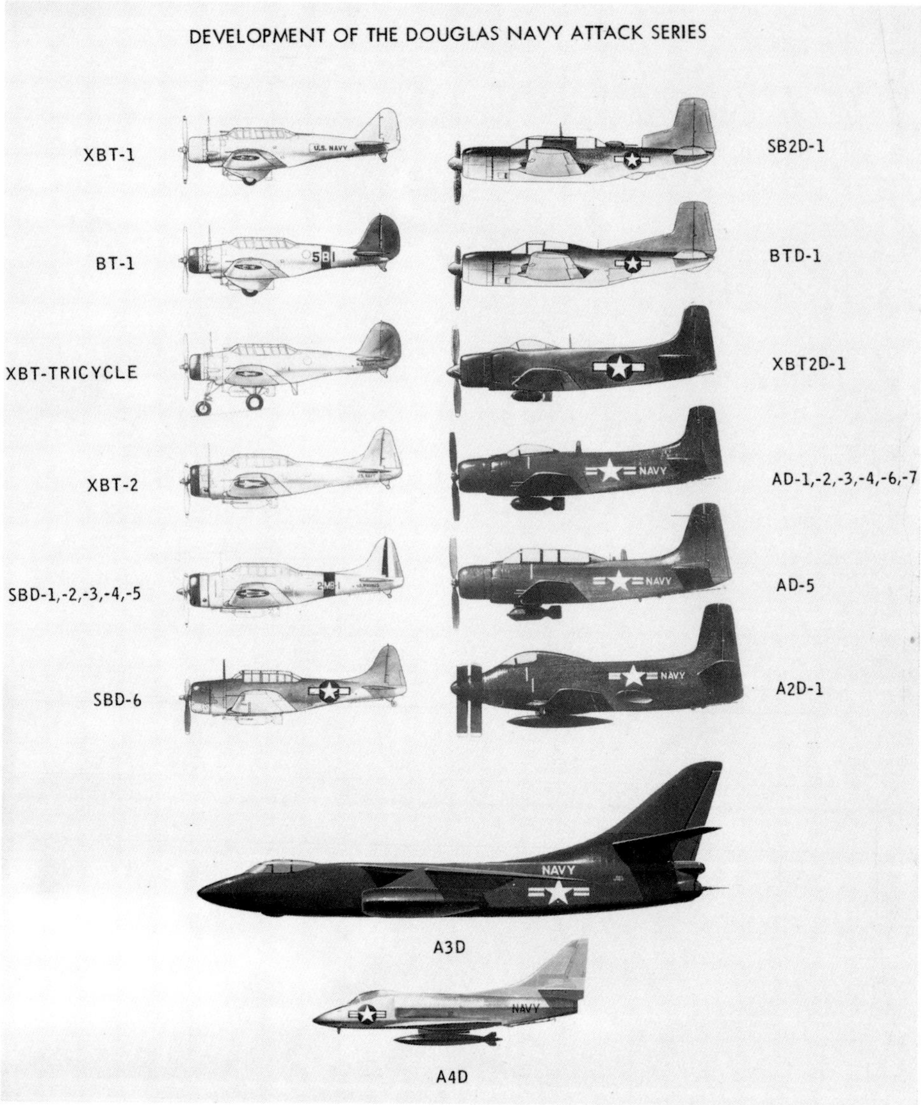


ABOVE: These drawings traced the progression of attack/bomber type aircraft at Douglas from the XBT1, top left, the first aircraft I worked on at Northrop/Douglas, to the A3D Skywarrior and A4D Skyhawk.

ABOVE LEFT: Another early drawing of the BT-1, this time in formation. (Provided by Harry Gann)

LEFT: Cutaway drawing of the BT2D-1, predecessor to the Skyraider, done in November, 1945.

Painting of BT-1s passing USS Ranger (CV-4)

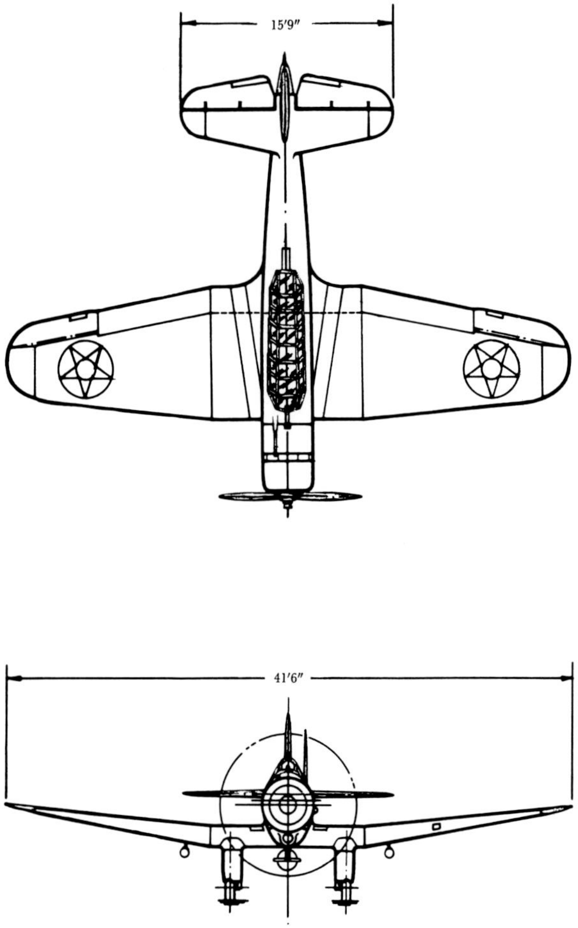


My first three-view drawings of the BT-1, 1930s. I was initially involved in the seat adjustment system on this plane.

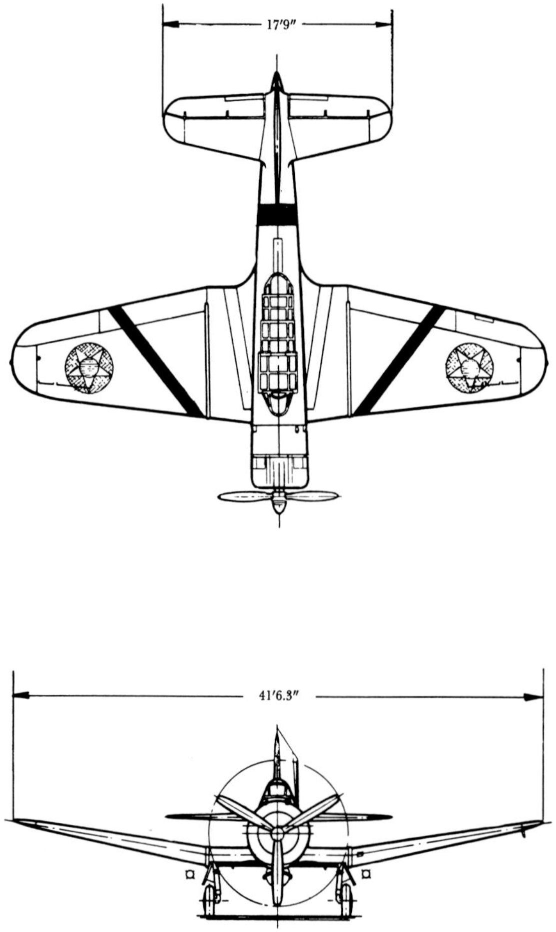


Three-view drawings of the SBD Dauntless, which played a key role in World War II combat.

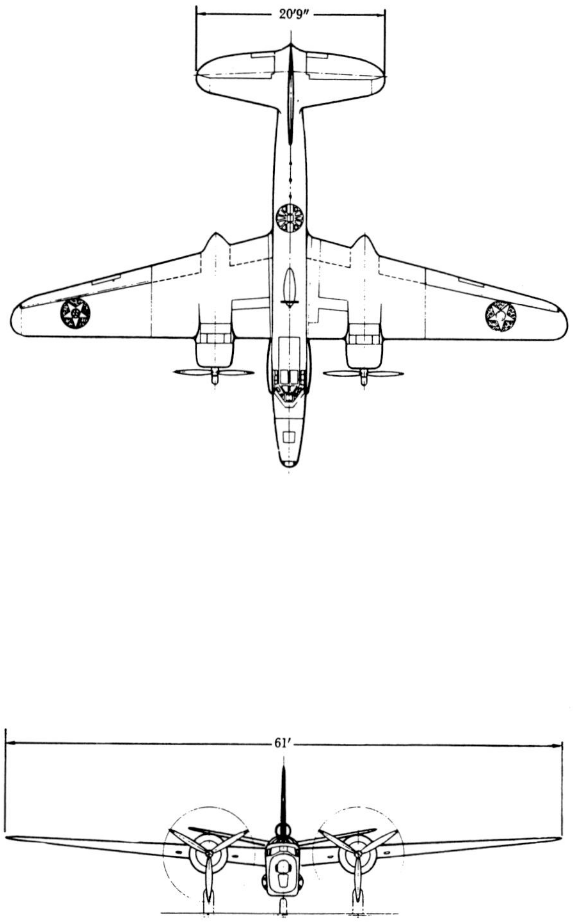


Model 7B was an early project at Douglas. It was first used by the French, and was later modified and evolved into the A-20 Havoc.

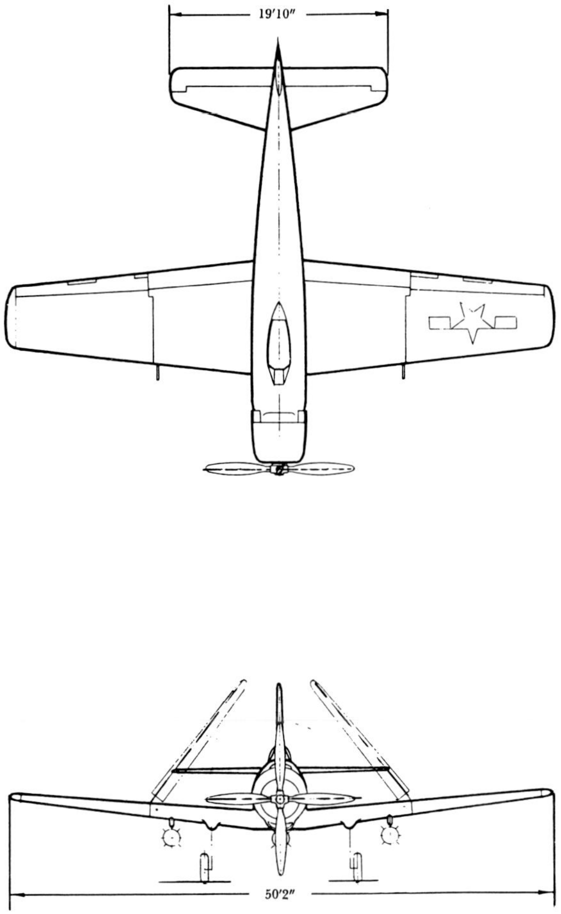


AD Skyraider was one of the greatest warplanes in the Navy, and later the USAF inventory.

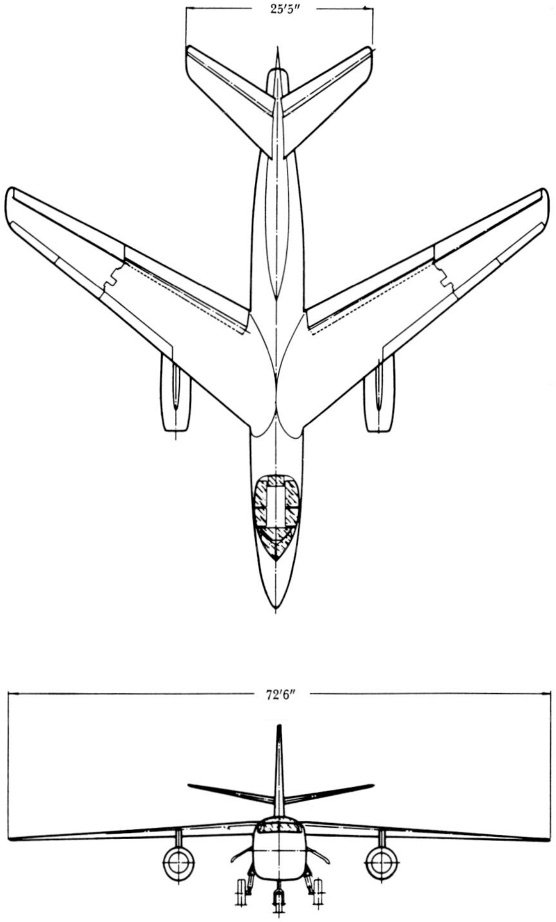


A3D Skywarrior came in well under 100,000 pounds, an outstanding achievement.

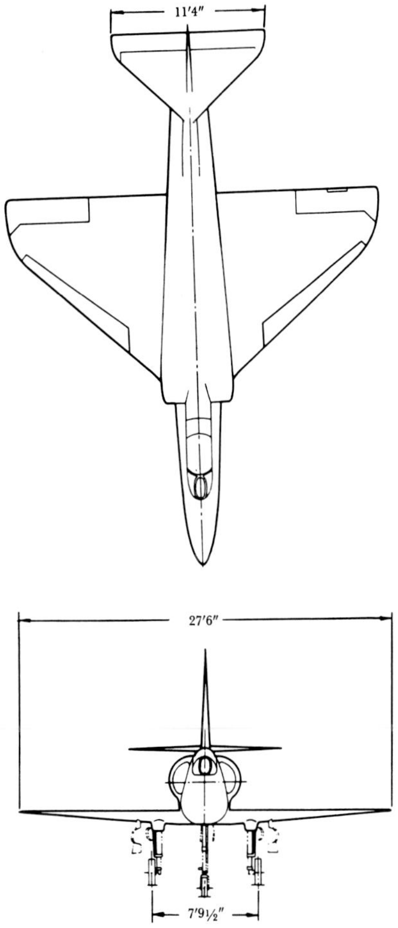


A4D Skyhawk was one of my favorites.

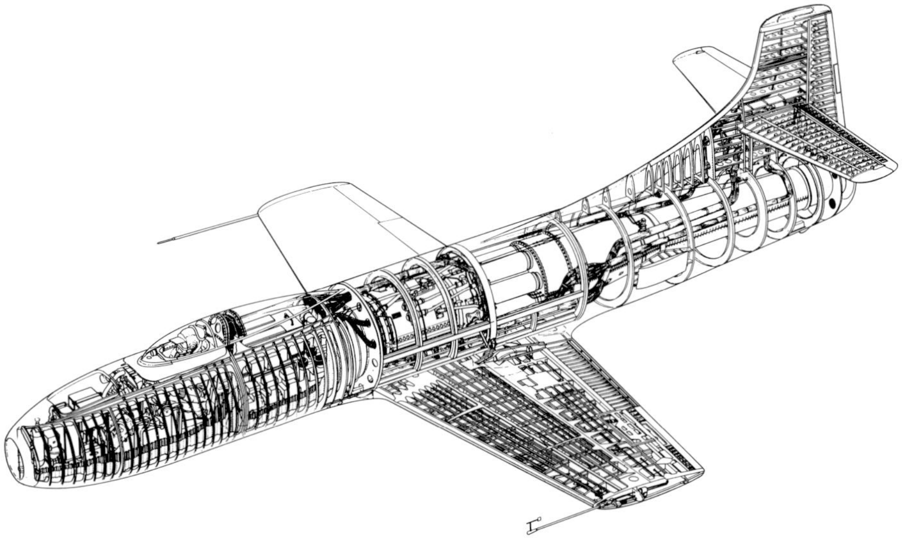

LEFT: Cutaway drawing of the Skystreak experimental aircraft.

BELOW: Detail drawing of F3D Skyknight.

BOTTOM: "The Crimson Test Tube," D558-1 Skystreak, in watercolor, used for promotional purposes.

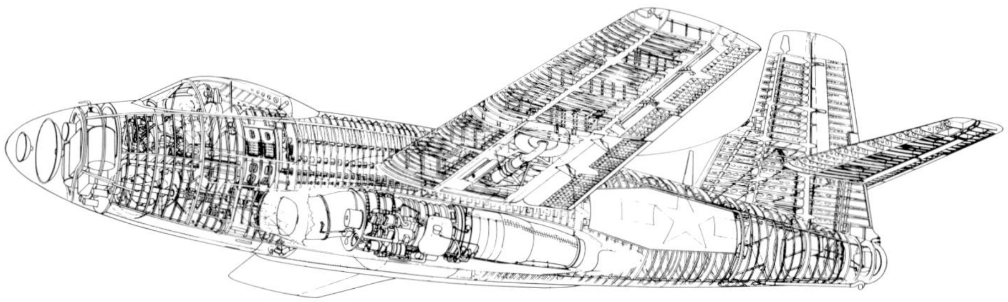

LEFT: F4D Skyray fighters had great climbing ability, which I tried to depict in this early work. Original is at Patuxent River, Maryland, site of Navy's flight test center.

BELOW LEFT: Original of this painting of Skyrays is also on display at Patuxent River, Maryland.

BELOW: I painted this mural of the D558-2 Skyrocket on 60 panels in a room 14 feet wide (my drawing board occupied 10 feet of the available space). It is mounted in the Naval Air Station Patuxent River Officers Club. It celebrated the Navy's first Mach II aircraft.

# modern aircraft

RIGHT: The Skyraider flew in the Korean and Vietnam War and is considered one of the best warplanes ever built.

BELOW: A4D Skyhawks on a Sandblower flight. Capable of delivering a nuclear weapon, Skyhawk pilots frequently practiced flying close to the ground.

BELOW RIGHT: Two-seat version of the Skyhawk.

A4F Skyhawks flying low.

OPPOSITE: These low-flying Skyhawks are loaded with bombs and rockets, and are on a Sandblower mission, a low-level, radar-evading flight, flown close to the ground. This image must have been popular, for the original was stolen and never found.

RIGHT: T-45 Goshawk training jets and their carrier seem to be chased by a thundershower.

BELOW: In this work I tried to convey the large size of the USAF's C-17 transport from a perspective behind the aircraft.

BELOW RIGHT: AV-8 Harriers, vertical takeoff and land jets flown by the Marine Corps, are depicted over a conceptual Sea Float operating base in a South Vietnamese river.

Grumman A-6 Intruders over a training base in the California desert.

F/A-18 Hornets over Yuma, Arizona.

RIGHT: T-45 Goshawks returning to the airfield.

BELOW: T-45 landing during student carrier landing qualifications.

BELOW RIGHT: F-4 Phantoms over a Southern California working (training) area.

OPPOSITE: Blue Angels fly over Statue of Liberty.

FOLLOWING PAGE: U.S. Marines in action. F/A-18 Hornets are depicted with LCACs – landing craft air cushion – vehicles, which skim above the surface of the water at high speed carrying troops and/or weapons and equipment from ships to shore.

1
2
3
4
5
6
U.S.NAVY
Blue Angels
R. G. Smith

MARINE

A-20B Havoc on the attack in the first raids in Europe in World War II by American pilots in American airplanes.

ABOVE: December 7th, 1941. The battleship, USS Nevada, gets underway after the Japanese attack on Pearl Harbor has begun. It was the only large ship to get under way during the attack.

ABOVE RIGHT: In May 1942, a furious naval battle erupted at Coral Sea. In this oil painting, titled "Coup de Grace," a TBD releases a torpedo against the Japanese carrier, Shoho, sinking the enemy ship. The Australians considered this battle their "Midway," the battle, a month later, which changed the course of the war in the Pacific. Lieutenant Commander Robert E. Dixon, the bomber commander on the TBD flight, radioed back to his carrier, USS Lexington, "Scratch One Flattop," one of the most memorable reports of World War II.

RIGHT: "Lady Lex Is Hit!" Oil. USS Lexington is fatally hit at the Battle of Coral Sea. "Lex" sank May 8, 1942.

OPPOSITE: "The Famous Four Minutes," is the title of this image. At the Battle of Midway in June, 1942, the U.S. Navy destroyed four enemy carriers, primarily with Douglas SBD dive bombers, and shot down a multitude of the enemy's best trained pilots. As a result, the American victory at Midway changed the course of the war in favor of the Allies. These SBDs, from USS Enterprise execute a fatal attack on the Japanese flattop, Akagi.

Another Battle of Midway view. SBDs successfully attack the Akagi, the only Japanese carrier with its island structure on the port side.

ABOVE: A TBD flown by Ensign George Gay approaches the Japanese carrier, Kaga, during the Battle of Midway, under intense anti-aircraft fire. His squadron skipper, Lieutenant Commander John Waldron, had ordered, "If there is only one plane left to make a final run-in, I want that man to go in and get a hit." Gay, as "tail-end Charlie," had watched all his squadron mates get shot down. In his attack, his gunner was killed, his plane damaged, and he crashed at sea. Gay actually watched the epic battle from the water and was rescued 30 hours later. He was the sole survivor of his flight.

ABOVE RIGHT: Admiral Arleigh Burke's Destroy Squadron 23 defeated a Japanese destroyer force in the early morning hours of November 25, 1943. This oil is titled, "The Little Beavers at the Battle of St. George."

RIGHT: F6F-5N Hellcats from VF(N)-41 damaged a Japanese destroyer they surprised on January 12, 1945, at dusk off the China coast north of Hong Kong. I was painting the scene, but didn't know the proper squadron markings. A fellow employee, Ken Smith, did. He also told me the pilot in the lead plane was Lieutenant William E. Henry, who worked for Douglas after the war. Pulling up after a run on the destroyer, Bill thought he had been hit due to a thudding sound beneath him. His wingman checked him over and reported that Bill had lost his centerline fuel tank on the pull-up. The metal straps which held the tank in place were flapping against the bottom fuselage. He was very relieved at the news.

U.S. paratroopers and supplies stream from Douglas-built C-47s during assault in European theater, World War II.

In "Berlin Airlift" I tried to convey the sense of terrible weather and busy activity our transport flyers had to contend with in Germany. A crisis was instigated by the Soviet Union when it blockaded the city in June 1948. The Russians hoped we would abandon West Berlin. But the Allies prevailed, supplying two million West Berliners with food and fuel for heating, an operation that continued until September 1949. Around-the-clock flights numbered 277,000, many made at three-minute intervals. Navy and Air Force flight and maintenance crews were key to the success of the effort.

ABOVE: In one of the most famous raids of the Korean War, AD Skyraiders from USS Princeton's VA-195 and VC-35, successfully struck the Hwachon Reservoir Dam, located just north of the 38th parallel. Here, the ADs climb away after the attack. The attack was led by Commander Swede Carlson.

ABOVE RIGHT: Korean War Skyraiders fly over burning tank, demonstrating the AD's outstanding close air support capabilities.

RIGHT: One of the most dramatic Yankee Station events was "wet-winging." In this case a Skyhawk makes it home, thanks to a Skywarrior tanker. Millions of dollars in aircraft costs were saved with this technique.

OPPOSITE: This is a fictional image of a Skyhawk delivering a nuclear bomb. The painting was done before the government imposed restrictions on graphically depicting explosions of nuclear weapons.

RIGHT: Commander T.R. Schwartz of USS Bon Homme Richard's VA-76 bags a MiG-17 over North Vietnam with a Zuni rocket, which had no guidance system and relied on the pilot for accuracy.

BELOW: This painting was titled, "Launch." An F-4 Phantom is about to be catapulted from a carrier, as Skyhawks, returning from a Vietnam combat mission, stream overhead and into the landing pattern.

BELOW RIGHT: OV-10s over South Vietnam.

ABOVE LEFT: Titled "Incident at Old Nam Can," this South Vietnam scene portrays an ongoing fire fight with U.S. patrol boats in foreground.

ABOVE: Aft gunner on station on patrol boat cruising the Vinh Te Canal in 1969.

LEFT: Swift boat speeding along in the Mekong Delta. This was a lithograph done for the Navy Department.

Grandson Steve Tack portrays F-14s during Desert Storm, in the Gulf War. I am very proud of his artistic skills.

RIGHT: On June 25, 1965, VA-25's Lieutenant Charlie Hartman, in the Skyraider on the left, and Lieutenant Clint Johnson in the second AD, bagged a MiG-17 during an engagement over North Vietnam, a headline-making event which produced a new level of respect for the prop-driven attack bomber.

BELOW: In this fictional image, an F/A-18 Hornet scores a kill on a Soviet Backfire fighter.

BELOW RIGHT: Commander, later Vice Admiral, Jim Stockdale, long-time prisoner of war and Medal of Honor hero in the Vietnam War, is in his VF-53 Vought Crusader in the foreground, with a Skyhawk and Skyraider in the distance. This oil portrays "Operation Pierce Arrow," August 5, 1964, the earliest American raid on North Vietnam shore targets. The petroleum storage facility at Vinh was set afire, and the 67-plane force inflicted considerable damage to other North Vietnamese shore installations. A Skyraider pilot was killed, an A-4 pilot shot down and captured on the raid.

# sketches

"Spotting on the Waist Cat." An A-4 Skyhawk on Yankee Station in the Gulf of Tonkin, loaded with rockets and bombs, is guided onto a waist catapult abeam the island of the carrier.

Witnessing flight operations aboard a carrier provided plenty of subject matter and opportunities to sketch scenes on the spot. In this one, "Hook Man," a sailor runs toward a jet which has landed, to free the hook when the fighter rolls aft slightly, loosening the hook's grip on the arresting cable.

F4D Skyray, as viewed from carrier's hangar deck, after jet has been lowered from flight deck level.

Flight deck crew relaxes alongside base of island in between launch and recovery period aboard carrier.

Regularly scheduled evening event was showing of a movie in the ready room. I sketched this view from the back row of a ready room.

In this finished drawing, A3D Skywarrior approaches cross-deck pendants (arresting cables) for landing, while, in the background, an ever-present Soviet trawler eyes U.S. flight operations.

RIGHT: A-1H/J single-seat version of the Skyraider leads multi-place A-1E version.

BELOW: In the 1950s, multi-crewed airborne early warning "Guppy" version of Skyraider (pod underneath contained radar), leads early "straight" version of the AD.

BELOW RIGHT: TBD Devastators of World War II were torpedo planes.

ABOVE: SBD Dauntless earned its stars at Battle of Midway, June, 1942.

ABOVE RIGHT: VFAW-3 F4D Skyray. The "bat wing" fighter was the first carrier-based delta-wing aircraft and served as an interceptor and fleet defense fighter. Between 1953 and 1958, it set seven world speed records. Harry Gann saw me painting the color version of this sketch using blue instead of the proper black color for the upper portion. Harry corrected me, thus learning of my vision's "gray-green weakness."

RIGHT: Skyhawks were in production at Douglas for 26 years. Here are three of the many versions, the A-4M in foreground, TA-4F two-seater in the middle, and the XA4D, the earliest version.

Drawing of aircraft carrier, USS Intrepid.

# civilian aircraft

RIGHT: My grandson, Steve Tack, is a terrific artist, as seen in his painting of a DC-3 ready to roll with Palm Springs, California, background. Steve called it, "Takeoff for Two," as a wedding gift to his sister, Kristy.

BELOW: DC-3 mail plane. The DC-3 (Air Force C-47, Navy R4D) aircraft has had a long, eventful life as one of the greatest transport aircraft in history.

BELOW RIGHT: DC-3 flying "over the hump" in Burma during World War II.

LEFT: Conceptual, short-takeoff-and-land aircraft designed by McDonnell Douglas.

BELOW LEFT: C-9 Skytrain II, built by McDonnell Douglas, flies over San Francisco's Golden Gate Bridge as a Navy carrier heads out to sea, below.

BELOW: DC-10 passes over Mount Rushmore, South Dakota.

Swissair DC-10. Notice, I included a Swissair DC-3 forward at a lower altitude.

DC-9 Super 80 version. DC-9 was the most successful of the company's commercial aircraft.

C-9 over New York's Statue of Liberty.

DC-9 Super 80 over towering clouds.

DC-9 of Toa Domestic Airlines (now Japan Air System) over Mount Fuji.

ABOVE: U.S. Navy C-9B, also called the Skytrain II, has been a reliable transport for many years.

ABOVE RIGHT: Formation of McDonnell Douglas "greats." In foreground, DC-10; in middle, DC-8; and lastly, DC-9.

RIGHT: DC-10 with Zaire's markings.

LEFT: DC-8 Super 63.

BELOW LEFT: DC-10 with United Airlines paint scheme.

BELOW: DC-10 wearing Egypt Air markings over the pyramids.

A Douglas C-1 refuels in flight an Atlantic (Fokker) C-2A Tri-Motor, circa 1927, during an endurance flight.

VMA-312 F4U Corsair, flown by USMC Captain Phillip DeLong, bags a Soviet-built YAK over North Korea on April 12, 1951. DeLong was a World War II ace, shooting down 11 enemy planes in that conflict. Actually, the squadron was designated VMF-312 at the time. Its new designation came a little later after this painting was completed.

Great early fighter was Boeing F4B-3, like this one from the Tophatters, based aboard USS Saratoga in background.

In the 1930s, Naval Aviation featured seaplanes, like this SOC-1. As airborne observers, they were the "eyes of the fleet." They were catapulted from ships then landed alongside after flight to be hoisted aboard.

PBY Catalina flying boat was a mainstay in the Naval Aviation arsenal in World War II.

These SBC-4 Scout Bombers of VS-2 were based on USS Lexington (CV-2) in the 1930s.

"War in the Air." B-17 Flying Fortresses are opposed by Fock-Wulfe 190s. This painting was the cover for a Time-Life book, "Americans in the Air War."

OPPOSITE: Bell X-1, with Chuck Yeager at the controls, is released by B-29 for supersonic flight. Third aircraft is a chase plane.

521800
6062
485004

Douglas-built heavy cargo transport, C-124 Globemaster, flies over Navy R4D (DC-3) at the South Pole. The R4D was the first aircraft to land at the Pole. Its seven-man Navy crew were the first to stand at the spot since Captain Robert F. Scott of England.

OPPOSITE: Called "SBDs in the Sun," this view features the distinctive swiss-cheese dive flaps on the SBD Dauntless which enabled it to make vertical dives on enemy shipping, enhancing accuracy of bomb drops, in World War II.

Blue Angels make low pass during air show.

Blue Angels in echelon. Each of the type aircraft the Navy's Flight Demonstration Squadron has flown since its inception from 1946 to the present is shown. From the top: F6F Hellcat, F8F Bearcat, F9F Panther, F9F Cougar, F11F Tiger, F-4 Phantom, A-4 Skyhawk and F/A-18 Hornet.

63

"The Fustest with the Mostest," is the title of this view of the Navy's first carrier USS Langely (CV-1) and the nuclear-powered USS Nimitz (CV-68). The phrase is derived from Civil War jargon.

OPPOSITE: Battlelship USS Missouri at sunset, an oil done in 1985.

While watching flight operations from the catwalk on board USS Midway, operating off the Aleutians in bad weather, I saw this A-6 Intruder emerge from low clouds. I asked pilots nearby, "If I painted this, what should I call it." One of them said, "On the Ball," meaning the aircraft was on glide slope as indicated by the glowing yellow light centered on the landing signal mirror located at the aft end of the carrier on the port side. So I named it, "On the Ball."

OPPOSITE: A-4 Skyhawks return from a mission to their flattop, the nuclear-powered carrier, USS Enterprise.

SR-71 high-altitude reconnaissance aircraft prowls the night skies over Canadian landscape.

P-3 Orion maritime patrol aircraft on the flight line at NAS Adak, Alaska. I called this one, "Even the Birds Are Walking."

In "Approaching Storm," USS Windham County is at Danang with bad weather looming nearby. This oil was a cover for U.S. Naval Institute Proceedings magazine.

LEFT: Orbital workshop, circa 1965.

BELOW LEFT: McDonnell Douglas didn't win the space shuttle contract, as proposed in this painting, but the paint scheme was used by the winning contractor because of its accuracy and adherence to specifications.

BELOW: "Project Apollo", 1965.

# other subjects

RIGHT: Pencil sketch, Long Beach Harbor, 1965. Note oil derricks in background.

BELOW: "Day's End," a watercolor scene, San Pedro. This was done "en plein air" which translates to "completed on location."

BELOW RIGHT: "Parallel Parking," Terminal Island, San Pedro, watercolor. A fishing boat prepares to go fishing. The orange truck is loaded with fuel. Also done "en plein air."

LEFT: Felt pen drawing, "Aunt Maude's Pad." This is the house Uncle Will built for his wife, my Aunt Maude. One day, Uncle Will went out for a haircut and never returned. Until the day she died, Aunt Maude refused to sell the house to developers. It began to lean with age and was eventually surrounded by apartment buildings.

BELOW LEFT: Sketch of abandoned building, Jerome, Arizona, 1993.

BELOW: Sketch of abandoned house done with felt pen, Auburn, California, 1950.

This oil painting of Indians in the desert is called, "A Gathering of Eagles." Because of my physical limitations, it is my last work of art. In fact, the painting is still incomplete.

RIGHT: "Carlton's Claim." Oil. My experience as a youth inspired a life-long interest in gold-mining scenes.

BELOW: "Changing Seasons," a forest scene. My daughter wanted a scene of the changing colors of the seasons to match the autumn colors in her family room.

BELOW RIGHT: "Little Toot." A tug boat motors along a tranquil Long Beach Harbor.

R.G. Smith

R.G. Smith

"Storm's A Brewin'," Nevada. This was an award-winner, painted from a sketch of the road behind the main street in Virignia City, Nevada, a location I often visited with sketch book in hand, circa 1950. Watercolor in tempera.

OPPOSITE: Left, charcoal drawing, "Monique." Right, "Amber," a pastel.

ABOVE LEFT: "Monterey Fisherman," my first oil, done in 1952, was based on an exercise done with water-color technique.

ABOVE: "Lighthouse At Point Vincente," Portugese Bend, California, an oil done in 1955.

LEFT: "Blue Door Adobe." I am an ardent admirer of the artist, Nicolai Fechin. Shortly after Fechin's death in 1955, while traveling through Taos, I visited the home of Fechin's daughter, Eya, to view some of her father's famous works. While there I made many sketches of the surrounding area. The "Blue Door Adobe," an abandoned Hopi dwelling, done circa 1966, evolved from these sketches.

"Sunset in Grant's Pass." I painted this when visiting old friends Marge and Bob Poole in Oregon.

An abandoned mine in oil titled, "Mojave Sunset."

OPPOSITE: "Market Place in Danang," is based on my "tour" in South Vietnam.

Oil called, "Vietnamese Girl."

Sketch of a commanche.

"The Old Cheyenne," color sketch, 1994.

ABOVE: Watercolor, "Coffee Break," Long Beach Harbor. Done "en plein air."

ABOVE RIGHT: "Paguate Watchtower," a sketch. Structure was a defense from roaming Navahos.

RIGHT: "Ghost Riders in the Sky." Watercolor. I saw horses in the clouds.

"Seen Better Days," watercolor, Terminal Island, San Pedro.

This watercolor, "Rust Bucket," done at San Pedro, has been popularly received over the years. A rusty freighter is bathed in 20 minutes of bright afternoon light during which the hull gained a special luster. Once the sun's descent continued, however, the light was gone and the ship became a rusty freighter again. Arthur Beaumont taught us that the right light doesn't last very long. The artist must catch it at the proper time and be ready.

ABOVE: “Albacore Haul,” Van Camp’s Tuna Factory, Terminal Island, San Pedro, watercolor. OPPOSITE: “High in the Sunlit Silence.” Oil.

# Epilogue

Above, left to right: sketching patrol boat, South Vietnam; on patrol, South Vietnam; 40° below zero, USS Midway; Blue Angel ride, 1979.

The fact that this story of a great American ever made it into print is a near miracle, because R.G. Smith is a truly quiet man. His modesty is as innate to him as his rare, God-given gifts of mind, eye, and hand.

As an aircraft engineer, he helped launch the historic evolution in military aircraft design and performance, beginning in the 1930s – literally, from "jennys" to jets. A talent for flawless perspective and intricate detail in line drawings and sketches led to a parallel career, which propelled him into becoming one of the top aviation artists of this or any other time. The works of others are often measured against those of R.G. Smith, and he has generously mentored several budding artists into careers of their own. But it doesn't stop there. Many of his presentations of land and seascapes, old mining camps, and Native American portraits are beyond stunning. They are priceless masterworks!

R.G. has gracefully blended two distinguished careers into a life's work, earning him countless formal honors in both the art and the military aviation worlds – with special esteem and acclaim from the Naval Aviation community – but he would never be the one to mention such recognition.

As members of a group of Naval Aviators privileged to have shared many hours with R.G. – whether in the western deserts scratching for gold during the day and telling yarns around the campfire at night, at aviation gatherings, or at special exhibits of his art work – whatever the setting, we always found him to be the same person, be it in a tuxedo, casual wear, or boondock grubbies. It goes without saying that R.G. was far more at home in the latter garb.

As for getting the rascal into his tux, we recall an elaborate subterfuge to have him suited up for a black tie awards banquet at the Annual Reunion and Symposium of the Marine Corps Aviation Association (MCAA) held at the Anaheim Marriott Hotel in October 1987. We couldn't risk telling him he was to be one of the select few to receive the MCAA Fighting Hawk Award. His wife, Betty, was in on the play, and she managed to get him there without revealing the real purpose. R.G. was clearly shocked when he was called to the stage, and appeared to be overwhelmed by being so honored. This is a genuinely HUMBLE man!

During campfire sessions, R.G. would listen closely and always enjoyed the aviators' tales of blood and thunder. Sometimes, after a few sips of quality bourbon, we just might draw out a yarn or two from him, which we yearned to hear. But he preferred to be a listener.

Sharing our love for aviation and the great outdoors, R.G. calls our group "the boys," and wears his respect for our military service on his sleeve. What he neither understands nor accepts is that HE is OUR hero. He might even become upset if he were to discover that we are sneaking these words of deep admiration into his own book.

Finally, "the boys," for whom I speak, wonder how much pressure (a tot of that fine bourbon, perhaps?) was required to persuade R.G. to finally tell his own story. Whatever it took, we are grateful and excited that his autobiography – at least in part – has finally been written.

Jay W. Hubbard
Brigadier General, USMC (Ret.)
Laguna Niguel, California, 1998